Promises, Promises

Promises, Promises

BOOK BY

Neil Simon

BASED ON THE SCREENPLAY

THE APARTMENT

BY BILLY WILDER & I. A. L. DIAMOND

MUSIC BY

Burt Bacharach

LYRICS BY

Hal David

Random House · New York

PROMISES, PROMISES *was first presented on December 1, 1968, by David Merrick at the Sam S. Shubert Theatre in New York City, with the following cast:*

(In order of appearance)

CHUCK BAXTER	Jerry Orhback
J. D. SHELDRAKE	Edward Winter
FRAN KUBELIK	Jill O'Hara
BARTENDER EDDIE	Ken Howard
MR. DOBITCH	Paul Reed
SYLVIA GILHOOLEY	Adrienne Angel
MR. KIRKEBY	Norman Shelly
MR. EICHELBERGER	Vince O'Brien
VIVIEN DELLA HOYA	Donna McKechnie
DR. DREYFUSS	A. Larry Haines
JESSE VANDERHOF	Dick O'Neill
DENTIST'S NURSE	Rita O'Connor
COMPANY NURSE	Carole Bishop
COMPANY DOCTOR	Gerry O'Hara
PEGGY OLSON	Millie Slavin
LUM DING HOSTESS	Baayork Lee
WAITER	Scott Pearson
MADISON SQUARE GARDEN ATTENDANT	Michael Vita
DINING ROOM HOSTESS	Betsy Haug
MISS POLANSKY	Margo Sappington
MISS WONG	Baayork Lee
BARTENDER EUGENE	Michael Vita
MARGE MACDOUGALL	Marian Mercer
CLANCY'S LOUNGE PATRONS	Carole Bishop, Rita O'Connor, Julane Stites, Rod Barry, Gene Cooper, Bob Fitch, Neil Jones, Scott Pearson, Michael Shawn
CLANCY'S EMPLOYEES	Graciela Daniele, Betsy Haug, Margo Sappington

41286

HELEN SHELDRAKE	Kay Oslin
KARL KUBELIK	Ken Howard
NEW YOUNG EXECUTIVE	Rod Barry
INTERNS AND THEIR DATES	Barbara Alston, Graciela Daniele, Gerry O'Hara, Michael Shawn
ORCHESTRA VOICES	Kelly Britt, Margot Hanson, Bettye McCormick, Ilona Simon

Directed by Robert Moore
Musical Numbers Staged by Michael Bennett
Settings Designed by Robin Wagner
Costumes Designed by Donald Brooks
Lighting by Martin Aronstein
Musical Direction and Dance Arrangements by Harold Wheeler
Orchestrations by Jonathan Tunick
Associate Producer: Samuel Liff

Synopsis of Scenes

Act One

Act Two

Musical Numbers

Overture

Act One

"Half As Big As Life"	CHUCK
"Upstairs"	CHUCK
"You'll Think of Someone"	FRAN, CHUCK
"Our Little Secret"	CHUCK, SHELDRAKE
"She Likes Basketball"	CHUCK
"Knowing When to Leave"	FRAN
"Where Can You Take a Girl?"	DOBITCH, KIRKEBY, EICHELBERGER, VANDERHOF
"Wanting Things"	SHELDRAKE
"Turkey Lurkey Time"	VIVIEN, MISS POLANSKY, MISS WONG

Act Two

"A Fact Can Be a Beautiful Thing"	CHUCK, MARGE, BAR PATRONS
"Whoever You Are"	FRAN
"A Young Pretty Girl Like You"	CHUCK, DR. DREYFUSS
"I'll Never Fall in Love Again"	FRAN, CHUCK
"Promises, Promises"	CHUCK

Act One

Scene 1

CHUCK BAXTER *is at his desk working at an adding machine. He looks up and notices the audience.*

CHUCK The main problem with working as a hundred-and-twelve-dollar-a-week accountant in a seventy-two-story insurance company with assets of over three billion dollars that employs thirty-one thousand two hundred and fifty-nine people here in the New York office alone . . . is that it makes a person feel so God-awful *puny.* (*He resumes work, then stops*) Not that I don't have aspirations and ambitions. I definitely have aspirations and ambitions . . . As you can see it's five-forty and everyone else went home at five-thirty and I didn't go home at five-thirty because Mr. Sheldrake, the personnel manager, doesn't leave until five-forty and I thought it wouldn't hurt, promotion-wise, if he saw me working past five-thirty—(SHELDRAKE *enters, heading for the elevators; he rings the elevator bell*) Evening, Mr. Sheldrake . . . How are you, Mr. Sheldrake . . . You're looking well, Mr. Sheldrake . . . (SHELDRAKE *enters the elevator*) Nice seeing you again, Mr. Sheldrake. Good-by, Mr. Sheldrake. (SHELDRAKE *has gone. Crossing in front of the desk,* CHUCK *sits against it*) If you've noticed, I'm the kind of person that people don't notice . . . I wish I were sitting out there with you so I could take a look at me and figure out what's wrong. (*He sings "Half As Big As Life"*)

Did you ever stop, really stop, and take a look
Take a look, a really good look at yourself?

I just took a peek, really peeked, to tell the truth
Through my eyes, I don't look so good to myself.

Half as big as life, that's me
But that's not the way I always mean to be.
Half as big as life, that's small
But deep in my heart I can feel
That I'm ten feet tall—ten feet tall.

I know that
Inside of myself there's a man, the kind of man
You would like, if you were just willing to look.

I've got lots of dreams
And my dreams will take me far
Very far, a cover is not the whole book.

Half as big as life, they say
But they're gonna see how wrong they are
Someday.
Half as big as life, that's small
But I wasn't born to be looked at
As five feet tall—no, not me.

I want a lot
And I know that I'll get it all
Just like someone who's
Twice as big as life.

(*He crosses behind the desk and puts on his jacket*) Not that there aren't some people around here who've noticed I'm something more than a nine-to-five adding machine . . . Like this real pretty girl who works up in the Employees' Cafeteria, Fran Kubelik . . . *she* notices . . . Oh, Miss Kubelik . . . Working late too, I see.

FRAN Oh, hello, Chuck. Yes, I had a few things to take care of in the cafeteria and I thought I'd just— Oh, what's the use, Chuck. I stayed late because I wanted to see you. I guess it's no secret that I'm enormously attracted to you but you never seem to pay any attention to me . . . Look, Chuck, can't we go somewhere and have a drink because—

CHUCK (*Raises his hand*) Wait! Hold it a second! (FRAN *freezes,* CHUCK *turns to the audience*) It's not true. She never said that. I mean, I can kid myself but there's no point in lying to you. I'm not doing too well in this department either. So sometimes I dream up conversations . . . (*He looks at her, then back to the audience*) Well, you can hardly blame me, can you? . . . No, what she actually said was—

FRAN Oh, hello, how are you, Frank?

CHUCK Chuck! Chuck Baxter.

FRAN Oh yes, I'm sorry.

CHUCK That's all right. How are things in the cafeteria?

FRAN Fine. I didn't see you there last week. Were you sick?

CHUCK No, I was there. You just didn't see me . . . Look, if you're not in a hurry to get home, I was wondering if—

FRAN Oh, excuse me, Chuck, I'm in a hurry to get home. Bye.
(*She exits into the elevator*)

CHUCK   —if you'd like to have a drink? (*To the audience*) How about you? You're not doing anything, are you? After work I usually like to unwind and have a friendly sociable drink at one of the bars on Second Avenue . . . where the young single set go . . . It could be any bar on Second Avenue . . . Your Mother's Hairnet, The Booze Boutique, Helen's Navel . . . As a matter of fact, my favorite Second Avenue bar is on First Avenue . . . It's owned by a friend of mine, Eddie Roth. (*The lights hit a sign that reads "Grapes of Roth." A bar is revealed, smoke-filled and packed with people. A dance is beginning.* CHUCK *enters the bar, and calls to the bartender*) Hi, Eddie. One beer!

> (BARTENDER EDDIE *draws a beer, which is passed from one customer to another, over the heads of the others, eluding* CHUCK. *When he finally gets it, a lady customer drops her cigarette in it. A well-dressed man in his early fifties fights his way through the crowd pulling an attractive girl with him*)

DOBITCH   Baxter! Baxter!

CHUCK   Oh, hello, Mr. Dobitch. (*To the audience*) Mr. Dobitch, an executive in the Mortgage and Loans Department, a very important man for me to know.

DOBITCH   Hya, Chuck. How are you?

CHUCK   Fine, Mr. Dobitch. What are you doing here? (*To the audience*) I'll tell you what he's doing here. Some married men between the ages of forty-five and fifty-five find single girls between the ages of twenty-one and thirty more attractive than some married women between the ages of forty-five and fifty-five, that's what he's doing here.

DOBITCH   Oh, just dropped in for a beer . . . Oh, Sylvia, I'd like you to meet a bright young man from our Accounting Department, Chuck Baxter. Chuck, I'd like you to meet Miss Gilhooley, a bright young girl from our Telephone Operating Department.

CHUCK   Hello.

SYLVIA   Pleased to make the connection. (*Aside to* DOBITCH) Mr. Dobitch, it's almost seven-thirty. Are we or aren't we?

DOBITCH   (*Aside*)   We are, we are—I'm trying, honey. (*To* CHUCK) Baxter, can I speak to you for a second? Man to man?

CHUCK   Gee, Mr. Dobitch, I never thought you considered me that way.

DOBITCH   (*Takes him aside*)   I've had my eye on you for a long time, Baxter . . . I understand you're a hard-working, dedicated, ambitious young man who has his own apartment on West Sixty-seventh Street. Is that true?

CHUCK   Well, I try, Mr. Dobitch.

DOBITCH   About the apartment?

CHUCK   Oh, that? Yes, it's true. I have a small place. One bedroom, nothing to speak about.

DOBITCH   I'd like to speak to you about it . . . The young lady I'm with is not feeling very well.

CHUCK   Oh, I'm sorry to hear that. Is there anything I can do?

DOBITCH Interesting you should ask. She'll be all right, you understand, but the thing is, she needs a place to lie down—for about forty-five minutes, an hour the most.

CHUCK Oh?

DOBITCH You see, she lives all the way up in the Bronx—

SYLVIA Brooklyn!

DOBITCH —all the way out in Brooklyn, and we have no place else to go . . .

CHUCK For what?

DOBITCH For her to lie down . . .

CHUCK I see what you mean, Mr. Dobitch. The thing is I was just going home. I'm learning to play tennis on Channel Thirteen and I was just getting to the point where my backhand . . .

SYLVIA (*For* CHUCK's *benefit, but poorly done*) Oh, God, am I feeling rotten.

DOBITCH She's feeling rotten.

CHUCK Well, I'm certainly not adverse to getting ahead, Mr. Dobitch, but you see, Mrs. Lieberman, the landlady, is very sensitive about bringing unattached young ladies up to the apartment—

DOBITCH She's not unattached. She's with me.

CHUCK   Oh! And you say she's really feeling sick?

DOBITCH   I just touched her hand. She's hot as a pistol.

CHUCK   (*Reaching in his pocket for the key*)   Well, if you think it won't be more than an hour.

DOBITCH   In her present condition, maybe only thirty minutes.

CHUCK   (*Hands him the key*)   Here's the key. Nineteen West Sixty-seventh Street, second floor front.

DOBITCH   (*Takes the key*)   I won't forget you for this, Baxter . . . advancement-wise.

CHUCK   There's some aspirins in the medicine cabinet and tea balls in the kitchen . . . Oh, and in case anything else develops, there's a doctor right next door.

DOBITCH   Bite your tongue, kid!
(*He exits with* SYLVIA. *Music begins. Everything blacks out except for a lone spotlight on* CHUCK)

CHUCK   (*Turning to the audience*)   As it turned out, he didn't need the doctor, the aspirin or the tea balls. He nursed her back to health with a bottle of vodka and my record player . . .

Fade Out

The outside stoop of a brownstone building swings in from the side.

CHUCK   She was fine the next day but it must have been a recurring ailment because she began feeling sick regularly every Tuesday night for the next month. But things were looking up. Mr. Dobitch introduced me to Mr. Kirkeby of Public Relations . . . (*Music to "Upstairs" begins*) . . . which meant that Wednesday nights I sat out in the public while he was busy having relations . . . (*He sings*)

> Upstairs—two flights up
> Looking out on the street
> For eighty-six fifty a month it's mine
> It may not be much but it's mine.
>
> You just go upstairs, two flights up
> Comfortable and complete
> For every-day living it works out fine
> It may not be much but it's mine.
>
> Except on Wednesday night
> It's walk, don't run.
> I just kill time till Mister Kirkeby's done
> With his Wednesday night fun
> Outside of that the place is mine.

> (*After* CHUCK *sings the first chorus,* GINGER *and* KIRKEBY *come out of the building.* CHUCK *hides behind the stoop*)

KIRKEBY Come on, Ginger, let's go.

GINGER Rush, rush, rush! First you rush me up here, then you rush me out.

KIRKEBY (*Looking at his watch*) I'm sorry, but I've got to meet my wife at eight-thirty. Tonight's our night with the marriage counsellor.
  (*Blackout; a spotlight turns on* CHUCK)

CHUCK Three weeks later, I still didn't have a promotion. However, I did meet Mr. Eichelberger of Research, who said he was looking for a bright young man for his department. He could have found one out on the stoop every Thursday night but he was busy doing research—upstairs, two flights up.
  (*The lights black out on* CHUCK *and go up on the apartment.* MR. EICHELBERGER, *a very austere, controlled-looking middle-aged executive, sits on the bed, wearing an opened vest, his head rests on his hands.* VIVIEN, *a nifty-looking brunette, sits near him*)

EICHELBERGER Oh, God, what have I done? I'm a married man with children, what kind of animal am I? A cheat, a liar, a phony. A deceiving sneak. *I've lost all respect for myself.*

VIVIEN What about next Tuesday?

EICHELBERGER Tuesday's *fine* with me.
  (*Blackout on the apartment; the lights go up on* CHUCK *in the vestibule outside his apartment*)

CHUCK And that's the way it went for a couple of months. Three nights a week I spend browsing through

Doubleday's, Brentano's, Cinema I, Cinema II, and once in *great* desperation, a dance at Hunter College. (*He bends down, lifts up the mat and picks up the key. He inserts it in the door*) Now you may ask the question, "Didn't I think lending out my apartment in hopes of getting a promotion was morally wrong?" (*He opens the door*) Well, my answer is— "Yes, but I tried not to think about it." (*He goes in and turns on the lights. He looks around the apartment, disgusted at the mess*) You'd think they'd have the decency to clean up afterwards. (*He picks up an empty liquor bottle*) I'm beginning to feel like a chambermaid in a New Jersey motel.

> (*He shakes his head angrily, then crosses to the door, opens it and puts out three empty bottles just as* DR. DREYFUSS, *an affable middle-aged man, comes up the vestibule heading for his own apartment directly opposite* CHUCK'S. *He carries the usual black bag*)

DR. DREYFUSS (*Disapproving*)   Hello, Baxter. And how is "Mr. Whoopee" today?

CHUCK   Oh, hi, Doc. Just tidying up.

DR. DREYFUSS (*Looks at the bottles*)   It's a wonder you can *stand* up. The garbage man told me the only place he picks up more empty bottles is the Copacabana.

CHUCK   That's not me, Doc. It's just that once in a while I have some people in for a drink.

DR. DREYFUSS   From what I hear through the walls, that's not all you have them in for. Three, four nights a week, you'll be dead by August.

CHUCK   I'm sorry if it gets noisy—

DR. DREYFUSS I was telling the interns at the clinic about you. Three of them want to study you, four of them just want to shake your hand.

CHUCK I'm afraid they'd be disappointed, Doc.

DR. DREYFUSS Yeah. Well, slow down, kid. Take some of those sleeping pills I gave you.

CHUCK I'm not tired.

DR. DREYFUSS Me! Me! I haven't closed an eye in six weeks.
(*He goes into his apartment.* CHUCK *goes back into his and closes the door*)

CHUCK Funny, isn't it? Everyone in the building thinks I'm the greatest lover in New York—and at Hunter I couldn't get a dance until "Goodnight, Sweetheart." (*Takes a pill*) Well, at least I'll get a night's sleep tonight.
(*The doorbell rings.* CHUCK *opens it.* MR. VANDER-HOF *stands there. He is another dapper middle-aged gentleman*)

VANDERHOF Baxter? C. C.?

CHUCK Yes?

VANDERHOF Hi there. Jesse Vanderhof, twenty-seventh floor, Claims Investigation. Ed Dobitch and Mike Kirkeby were talking about you the other day in the Executive Dining Room and I thought I'd just drop by to say hello.

CHUCK Oh, that's very nice of you, Mr. Vanderhof. Hello.

VANDERHOF Hello. (CHUCK *starts to close the door quickly.* VANDERHOF *grabs it*) Forty-five minutes, kid, that's all I need the place. I got very lucky this afternoon.

CHUCK (*Trying to shut the door*) Yeah, well, your luck ran out tonight because I just took a sleeping pill.

VANDERHOF Kid, you don't understand. This is a nurse. She works for my dentist. I only see him twice a year. I won't bother you again until April.

CHUCK I've heard that before.

VANDERHOF I just had a tooth pulled. Give me a break, kid, the Novocaine is wearing off.

CHUCK I've got my own health to think about. The last hot meal I had was a bag of roasted chestnuts.
     (*He closes the door and leans his back against it*)

VANDERHOF Baxter, there's a Junior Executive opening coming up in my department next month.

CHUCK (*Nothing doing*) Promises, promises, I'm sick and tired of promises.

VANDERHOF I'll put your name on top of the list.

CHUCK Is that a promise?

VANDERHOF It is not a promise, it's my bonded word of honor.

CHUCK (*Opens the door*) Well, as long as it's not a promise.

VANDERHOF (*Entering, circling from the sofa to the door*) You won't regret this, kid.

CHUCK You get the apartment just the way it is. I'm all out of liquor, all out of cheese, all out of crackers . . .

VANDERHOF Don't worry about it, I can't eat anything for an hour anyway.
> (*He goes into the hall and whistles, then returns to the apartment and starts to help* CHUCK *on with his raincoat*)

CHUCK (*Putting it on*) I don't know why you can't go to a motel.

VANDERHOF (*Softly*) Because no decent girl would go to a motel with a man she met three hours ago . . . A friend's apartment is different . . . Can't you put your coat on outside?
> (CHUCK *has an arm in one sleeve of his coat as* VANDERHOF *ushers him toward the door*)

CHUCK I don't know where you get your energy, Mr. Vanderhof. You should be home gargling with salt water. (*He steps to the hall and comes face to face with the willowy* NURSE) . . . Oh, hello.

NURSE I just dropped by to powder my nose.
> (*She slinks into the apartment.* VANDERHOF *comes out into the hall with* CHUCK)

CHUCK (*Whispers*) Well, tell her not to powder too loud. I've got neighbors, you know.
> (*He starts down the hall*)

VANDERHOF (*Calls after him*) If you can make it an hour and a half I'd appreciate it. (CHUCK *disappears as* VANDERHOF *goes into the apartment, closing the door behind him. At that moment,* DR. DREYFUSS *opens his door, putting out empty milk bottles.* VANDERHOF *says to* NURSE) . . . And now, Miss Kreplinski, shall we have a little music while we discuss my bridgework.

> (*He flips a record on the phonograph. Music comes on.* DR. DREYFUSS *listens, shakes his head and turns into his apartment*)

DR. DREYFUSS Mildred! He's at it again!

> (*The lights black out on* DR. DREYFUSS *and* VANDERHOF *and light up on* CHUCK *as he sits on the front stoop*)

CHUCK (*He is angry, but mostly with himself*) No, I am not altogether proud of myself, if that's what you're thinking . . . But let me tell you this . . . Once I get to be a Junior Executive, I am going to work harder and later and with more dedication than any Junior Executive who ever lent out his apartment ever did before . . . (*He looks up*) . . . and some day *I'm* the one who's going to be . . . (*Singing*)

> Upstairs two flights up
> Looking out on the street
> For eighty-six fifty a month it's mine
> It may not be much but it's mine.

> (*Lightning flashes, thunder rolls and* CHUCK *looks up as if to say "Wouldn't you know it." He lifts his collar up about his neck and sinks deeper into his coat*)

Fade Out

Scene 3

1ST GIRL (*On mike*) Good morning, Consolidated Life. I'm sorry, he's not in yet.

2ND GIRL (*On mike*) Good morning, Consolidated Life. No, he gets in at nine.

1ST GIRL (*On mike*) Good morning, Consolidated Life. Oh, hello, Ethel. Wasn't that some storm last night?
    (CHUCK *appears on the right and crosses to the center*)

CHUCK They didn't leave until two-thirty in the morning. Don't come near me, I'm very sick. (*To* NURSE) Er, my name is Baxter. I'd like to see the Doctor, please.

NURSE Do you have an appointment?

CHUCK No, just a cold. It was unexpected. I didn't know it was coming.

NURSE Take a seat, the Doctor will be right with you.

CHUCK I hope so, I'm almost out of nasal spray . . . By the way, I have a 101.3 temperature. You can see it on my thermometer here.
    (*He shows her the thermometer*)

NURSE The Doctor will take it.

CHUCK   Oh. (*He starts to give it to her*) All right. If I can have it back when he's through. It's my only thermometer . . .

NURSE   He has his own. Will you please sit down?
(*He sits as the* COMPANY DOCTOR *and* VANDERHOF *come out of the office*)

DOCTOR   I'd leave the bandage on another day, Mr. Vanderhof.

VANDERHOF   Right, Doc.

DOCTOR   And I don't care what you say, they still look like teeth marks to me.
(*He exits*)

CHUCK   Hi, Mr. Vanderhof.

VANDERHOF   Oh, hi, kid.

CHUCK   Don't "Hi, kid" me. Do you know I sat on a park bench until two-thirty in the morning in a snow storm in a London Fog coat? It's for fogs in London, not snow in New York!

VANDERHOF   I'm sorry, kid. By the way, I intend to pay you for the broken ironing board. Kind of interesting the way it happened.

CHUCK   And then you left the wrong key under the mat. I had to sleep in a Spanish Synagogue on Sixty-ninth Street.

VANDERHOF   Think about your promotion, kid. I spoke to Mr. Sheldrake in Personnel, you should be hearing from him this morning.

CHUCK   If I'm still alive.

VANDERHOF   Now put me down for the apartment next Friday. And get in some new records, will you? It's not easy being sexy to Lithuanian Folk Dances.
    (*Exits*)

CHUCK (*Shouts*)   No one's using anything until I hear from Mr. Sheldrake! (*He holds his head*) Oh, God, I cracked a sinus.
    (FRAN *enters*)

FRAN   Excuse me, is the Doctor in?

CHUCK (*Rising*)   Oh, Miss Kubelik, hello.

FRAN   Oh, hello, er—

CHUCK   Frank . . . er, Chuck. Chuck Baxter.

FRAN   Yes, I know. How are you?

CHUCK   Oh, just a little cold. How are you?

FRAN   Oh, the same old problem. Can't eat, can't sleep, just thinking about you, dreaming about you, hoping you'll call me—

CHUCK (*Turns to the audience*)   I'm sorry, I won't do that again. (*To* FRAN) And how are you?

FRAN   Oh, just a mild case of the hiccups.

CHUCK   I'm sorry, my Eustachian tubes are blocked up, I didn't hear what you said. (*She hiccups*) No, I heard that. I missed the part in front of it.

FRAN   I said just a mild case of hiccups.

CHUCK   Oh. (*He is stuck for a moment. To the audience*) I think I'm running out of conversation . . . I mustn't panic. If I keep talking I'll be all right. (*To* FRAN) So, you have a mild case of the hiccups, do you?

FRAN   Yes.

CHUCK   I see. (*To the audience*) That's it. I have no more thoughts, I'm finished.

FRAN   By the way, they made me hostess in the Executive Dining Room.
          (*She hiccups*)

CHUCK   I heard. Congratulations.

FRAN   So I guess I won't be seeing you any more in the cafeteria.

CHUCK   Unless I become an executive, which isn't entirely remote. Excuse me, a terrible sneeze is coming.
          (*He holds it in*)

FRAN   You really shouldn't suppress it, you know. You could blow out something internally. (*She hiccups*) Sneeze. (*He sneezes*) God bless you.

CHUCK   Thank you. (*She hiccups*) Hey, we had a nice rhythm going there.

FRAN   I don't know what brought these on.

CHUCK   I read that emotional distress can sometimes cause hiccups. Are your emotions by any chance distressed? I don't mean to pry.

FRAN   I don't think so.

CHUCK (*To the audience*)   I think so. There was talk she was involved with some man but it's over now . . . Don't say anything. (*To* FRAN) Listen, I'm not a doctor or anything, but why don't you try taking your mind off whatever it is that's distressing you.

FRAN   How?

CHUCK   Well, try thinking about something else—get involved with a new interest. (*To the audience*) Me, me! Please let it be me.

FRAN   Like what?

CHUCK   Like me! I mean, take a person like me. I have lots of interests . . . uh . . . walking . . . browsing . . . (*The music to "You'll Think of Someone" begins*) . . . Don't you have any hobbies?

FRAN   I don't like doing things alone.

CHUCK   Oh, well, I'm sure there are lots of interesting people who'd be interested in doing things with you . . . for example . . .

FRAN (*Singing*)

    I could take up knitting to feel better
    I'd make someone a hand-knit sweater
    But I just don't know who that someone should be.

CHUCK (*Singing*)

    If you can't think of anyone else
    How about maybe, someone
    Like for example, perhaps, someone
    Oh, you'll think of someone.

FRAN

    I could take up tennis to relax me
    A game of doubles wouldn't tax me
    But I just don't know who my partner should be.

CHUCK

    If you can't think of anyone else
    How about maybe, someone
    Like for example, perhaps, someone
    Oh, you'll think of someone

FRAN *and* CHUCK

    Who likes you and the things you like to do
    Happy little things like climbing hills
    And rowing boats on a lake
    Fun is something that is yours to take.

FRAN

    I could take up painting to amuse me
    A portrait picture might enthuse me
    But I just don't know who my model should be.

CHUCK

    You can bet that there's someone around

FRAN
　　Someone to talk to, laugh with
　　Like for example dance with, sing to . . .

CHUCK
　　Cling to . . .

　　(*The* NURSE *comes out of the office*)

NURSE　Baxter? Mr. Sheldrake in Personnel wants to see you right away. You're next, miss.

CHUCK　(*Excited*)　Did you hear that? Did you hear? This is what I've been waiting for in the fog and the snow and the cold for two months.

FRAN　Well, I wish you the best of luck. And I want to thank you for trying to help me. It was very nice of you, Chick.

CHUCK　Chuck.

FRAN　Oh, yes, I'm sorry . . . Well, I hope I'll be seeing you in the Executive Dining Room. Bye. (*She enters the office and the* NURSE *follows*)

CHUCK　(*He looks after her and sings*)
　　When you think about that someone
　　Who it could be
　　How about me?

Fade Out

Scene 4

The office of J. D. SHELDRAKE, *the Personnel Director. It is not an executive suite, but it is several pegs above the glass cubicles of the middle echelon.* MISS OLSON, *an attractive secretary, ushers* CHUCK *into the office.*

MISS OLSON If you'll take a seat, Mr. Sheldrake will be right with you.

CHUCK Thank you.
　　　(*He sits*)

MISS OLSON And relax.

CHUCK I'm perfectly relaxed. (*She smiles and exits. He turns to the audience*) We know better, don't we? (SHELDRAKE *enters*) Mr. Sheldrake? I was told you wanted to see me . . . C. C. Baxter . . . (SHELDRAKE, *smiling at* CHUCK, *sits, picks up a folder of papers from the desk and studies them*) . . . Premium Accounting Division . . . Baxter . . . C. C.?
　　　　　(SHELDRAKE *puts down the papers, sits back in his reclining chair, cups his hands under his chin and studies* CHUCK *in silence a moment.* CHUCK *fidgets nervously*)

SHELDRAKE So you're C. C. Baxter.

CHUCK (*Big smile*) Yes, sir. I am. I am C. C. Baxter.

SHELDRAKE Mmmm, hm.

CHUCK Yes, sir.
  (SHELDRAKE *looks at the papers again;* CHUCK *sniffles*)

SHELDRAKE Is that a cold you have there, Baxter?

CHUCK Where? Oh, here . . . (*He touches his nose*)
Yes, sir, that's a cold. I haven't been sleeping much lately.

SHELDRAKE Maybe you ought to go to bed early.

CHUCK That certainly is wonderful advice, Mr. Sheldrake
. . . The thing is, I've been trying to catch up on extra
work in the office a couple of nights a week. (*Turns to the
audience*) I've sold out. God'll punish me.

SHELDRAKE So you do have ambitions.

CHUCK Yes, sir, I do . . . Ambitions and capabilities . . .

SHELDRAKE Like "Loyal, resourceful, cooperative"?

CHUCK Well, yes, those are good ones.

SHELDRAKE (*He picks up the papers on his desk and
looks at them*) That's what Mr. Vanderhof thinks. This
is his report. He says you're loyal, resourceful, cooperative.

CHUCK (*He twists his head to look at the report*) Mr.
Vanderhof said that? In that order? Imagine.

SHELDRAKE And Mr. Dobitch told me that you've been
of immense help to him. And Mr. Kirkeby in Public
Relations thinks you're very bright.

CHUCK   Mr. Kirkeby thinks I'm bright?

SHELDRAKE   Yes, they're all keen on you. Vanderhof, Kirkeby, Dobitch . . . even Mr. Eichelberger.

CHUCK (*To the audience*)   I think they overdid it. He's going to want to know what makes me so popular.

SHELDRAKE   Tell me, Baxter, what makes you so popular?

CHUCK   Well, I imagine it's . . . Well, they probably . . . I don't know.

SHELDRAKE   Baxter, is it your impression that I'm stupid?

CHUCK   No, sir, it is not. Have I given the impression that you give that impression, sir?

SHELDRAKE   Well, I can tell you I'm anything but stupid. I know everything that goes on in this building. In every department, on every floor.

CHUCK (*To the audience*)   All right, don't get nervous. Because if you get nervous, I'll get nervous. (*To* SHELDRAKE) On every floor?

SHELDRAKE   In nineteen sixty-three we had an employee here named Fowler. Fowler was very popular too. Turned out he was running a bookie joint right in the Actuarial Department . . . tying up the switchboards, figuring the odds on our IBM machines. Used to pass the money back and forth on the coffee wagon. Winners paid off under the prune danish.

CHUCK   Isn't that terrible?

SHELDRAKE It was for Fowler. I let him keep the prune danish because I knew he wouldn't be eating again for a long time.

CHUCK Sir, is there some point in this story that you're trying to point out to me? Because I'm not running any bookie joint.

SHELDRAKE (*He stops behind him and speaks into his ear*) What kind of joint *are* you running?

CHUCK I, sir? Me?

SHELDRAKE There's a certain key floating around the office, from Kirkeby to Vanderhof to Eichelberger to Dobitch back to Kirkeby, et cetera, et cetera, et cetera. That key I mentioned is to a certain apartment . . . And do you know who that key belongs to?

CHUCK (*To the audience*) You are looking at a young man in big trouble. (*To* SHELDRAKE) Do you?

SHELDRAKE Yes.

CHUCK (*To the audience*) See?

SHELDRAKE To "Loyal, Resourceful, Cooperative C. C. Baxter." Can I get you anything? Coffee? Prune Danish?

CHUCK Mr. Sheldrake, if you would just let me explain—

SHELDRAKE All right.

CHUCK Oh! . . . Well, you see one night about two months ago I was on my way home from work when I

stopped in at the Grapes of Roth for a quick beer . . .
that's all I drink, quick beers . . . when I met a certain
executive from one of our departments, quite a decent
gentleman, who was suddenly confronted with this very
unusual problem—

SHELDRAKE   The girl he was with was feeling sick.

CHUCK   —the girl he was with was feeling sick. That's
right! . . . Anyway, you could see she was hot as a pistol
and all she needed was—

SHELDRAKE   A place to lie down.

CHUCK   —a place to lie down. You're right again. Anyway,
he was in a tight spot because this girl—

SHELDRAKE   Lived all the way up in the Bronx.

CHUCK   No, as a matter of fact, she lived in Brooklyn.

SHELDRAKE   Where did I make my mistake?

CHUCK   That's all right. So what could I do but give him
the key to my apartment? Then pretty soon I started
getting calls from these other decent executives and that's
pretty much how this whole thing sneaked up on me.
          (*He takes out a spray bottle and quickly sprays
          both nostrils*)

SHELDRAKE   Baxter, an insurance company can't afford to
betray the public trust, you agree with that?

CHUCK (*Grimaces*)   Ohhh.

SHELDRAKE   You don't agree?

CHUCK I agree. I just sprayed my nose with eye drops. That can't hurt me, can it? I mean, you can't go blind in the nose.

SHELDRAKE Baxter, how many charter members are there in this little key club of yours?

CHUCK Just those four. Out of a total of 31,259 employees . . . so percentage-wise, we can be very proud of our personnel . . . (*He sniffs, then breathes freely*) Gee, the eye drops are better than the nose drops.

SHELDRAKE That's not the point. Four rotten apples in a barrel, no matter how large the barrel . . . You realize that if this ever leaked out—

CHUCK Oh, it won't, believe me. And I've decided from now on no more apples are going to use my barrel . . . apartment. (*He squints*) I wonder if the ear drops would work in the eyes.

SHELDRAKE Where is it?

CHUCK What?

SHELDRAKE Your apartment.

CHUCK West Sixty-seventh Street . . . But I'm changing the key, the lock, the door. I'd change my name but I don't know how else I'd get my mail.

MISS OLSON (*Entering*) Excuse me. Mrs. Sheldrake called and wants to know if you'll be home for dinner.

SHELDRAKE No, tell her I'm taking the branch manager from Kansas City to the basketball game. I'll be home late.

MISS OLSON Yes, sir.
   (*She exits*)

SHELDRAKE Tell me something, Baxter. Do you like basketball?

CHUCK Basketball? I love it. I was going to play in college . . . but I stopped growing in high school.

SHELDRAKE How'd you like to see the Knicks' first game tonight?

CHUCK You mean you and me? Well, won't the branch manager from Kansas City be disappointed . . . ?

SHELDRAKE I made other plans for him . . . and me. You can have both tickets.

CHUCK Well, that's very kind of you . . . but I thought I'd just go home and take some Excedrin, Bufferin, Contac, Dristan, Cope, a lot of that stuff . . .

SHELDRAKE You don't understand, Baxter. I'm not just giving you these tickets . . . I want to *swap* them.

CHUCK Swap them? What could I have that you would possibly want?

SHELDRAKE (*He picks up* VANDERHOF's *report*) It also says here that you are alert, astute and quite imaginative.

CHUCK Well, I am but I just can't imagine— (*The dawn breaks*) Oh! (*He reaches into his pocket and takes out the key*) This?

SHELDRAKE (*Smiles*) . . . And I see what they mean . . . Next week there's going to be a shift in personnel around here, and as far as I'm concerned, do you know what I think you are?

CHUCK Executive material?

SHELDRAKE We think alike. Now put down the key— (CHUCK *quickly puts the key on the desk.* SHELDRAKE *pushes a pad toward* CHUCK)—and put down the address.
(CHUCK *grabs the thermometer, lays the key on the desk, unclips what he thinks is his pen and starts to write on the pad*)

CHUCK It's the second floor front . . . my name's not on the door . . . it just says 2A . . . and the "A" fell off . . . (*Suddenly realizes he's writing with his thermometer*) Oh, that's my thermometer . . . (*Looks at it*) 106? My God . . . (*Then realizes*) Oh, that's just my pocket temperature . . .

SHELDRAKE Relax, Baxter.

CHUCK Thank you, sir. I certainly will.
(*He replaces the thermometer with his pen and resumes writing*)

SHELDRAKE Now remember, Baxter, what is tonight going to be?

CHUCK Tonight, sir? (*Thinks*) A fun evening?

SHELDRAKE No, Baxter. Tonight is going to be our little secret.

CHUCK   Oh, of course. You didn't even have to say that.

SHELDRAKE   You know how people talk.

CHUCK   You don't have to remind me.

SHELDRAKE   Not that there's anything wrong. This happens to be a nice girl.

CHUCK   Listen, you didn't have to tell me. Besides, it's none of my business. I mean, after all, four apples, five apples, what's the difference?

SHELDRAKE   That's where you're wrong, Baxter. From now on there's only room for one apple in the basket, right?

CHUCK   Right.
        (CHUCK and SHELDRAKE sing "Our Little Secret")

CHUCK
        All the other apples are spoiled and they're rotten
        Out of the basket they'll go.

SHELDRAKE
        Your loyalty is something that won't be forgotten.

CHUCK
        And there's one thing I promise you
        I can keep secrets, too.
        Oh—

CHUCK and SHELDRAKE
        It's our little secret
        Little secret, little secret . . .

CHUCK
> I'm gonna buy me a hat
> And keep our secret under that.

CHUCK *and* SHELDRAKE
> It's our little secret
> Little secret, little secret . . .

CHUCK
> I'll even stop counting sheep
> To prove I don't talk when I sleep.

CHUCK *and* SHELDRAKE
> We've got a little plot
> That we can tell—just one another
> There isn't anyone
> That we can trust, except each other.

> That's why we'll never tell a soul
> What it's all about
> They'll never get a chance
> To find out.

SHELDRAKE
> There'll be questions

CHUCK
> I won't answer

SHELDRAKE
> There'll be gossip

SHELDRAKE *and* CHUCK
> Let them gossip
> We don't care.

CHUCK
> Just put your trust in me.

CHUCK *and* SHELDRAKE
> It's our little secret
> And I'll keep it locked inside me
> 'Cause it's no one else's business
> But our own anyhow . . .

> > (MISS OLSON *enters.* CHUCK *and* SHELDRAKE *whistle four bars.* MISS OLSON *exits*)

> 'Cause it's no one else's business
> But our own anyhow.

> Our little secret, oh yes, it's yours and mine
> Our little secret, for now and all the time
> We'll stick together
> 'Cause we've got our little secret now.

> > (*After the number is over there is a blackout on the set, except for a spot that stays on* CHUCK *as he steps out front and addresses the audience*)

CHUCK   Listen, I wouldn't be too quick to judge a decent executive like Mr. Sheldrake. . . . I wouldn't want to pin any labels on him like "hypocritical" or "unprincipled." No, sir, not me . . . Of course, *you're* free to make up your own minds.

Fade Out

SCENE 5

CHUCK *waits in the lobby of Consolidated Life as other employees emerge, some posting letters on their way home.* FRAN *passes him on her way to the letter box.*

FRAN (*She passes* CHUCK) Good night.

CHUCK Good night . . . Oh, hey, Miss Kubelik, I've been waiting for you.

FRAN You have?

CHUCK I almost didn't recognize you without your hiccups. I don't hear them so I guess you cleared up your emotional distress.

FRAN Well, temporarily. Did you get your promotion?

CHUCK Table for one tomorrow in the Executive Dining Room. And I like my salad tossed from left to right.

FRAN Good. Congratulations.

CHUCK Thanks. (*She starts toward the revolving door*) Oh, Miss Kubelik. Look, is there a wild, way-out remote impossible possibility that you'd be interested in basketball?

FRAN Oscar Robertson led the N.B.A. in scoring last year with a twenty-nine-point-seven average.

CHUCK That's right! Even the point seven. How did you know that?

FRAN I live in three and a half rooms with a father, brother, and one television set.

CHUCK   Well, how'd you like to see the Knicks play in actual, real-life seven-foot-tall flesh?

FRAN   You mean tonight?

CHUCK   (*He takes the tickets out*)   Yes.

FRAN   I'm sorry, I can't tonight. I'm meeting someone.

CHUCK   Oh. Exit the hiccups, heh? This date . . . is it just a date . . . or is it something serious . . . I'm sorry, you don't have to tell me that.

FRAN   It *used* to be serious . . . At least *I* was, he wasn't.

CHUCK   He must be crazy . . . So where does it stand now? You really don't have to answer that.

FRAN   I don't know where it stands. I'm just going to have a drink with him. He's been calling me all week.

CHUCK   He must be a nice fellow if you're interested in him.

FRAN   I'm not interested in him. I'm interested in you. I've always been interested in you. You're all I ever think about or dream about or—

CHUCK   (*He yells at himself*)   All right, cut that out, Chuck. (FRAN *freezes*) No one's interested in what you *want* to hear. (*To the audience*) You're interested in what she *said*, right? And what she said was—

FRAN   (*Unfreezes*)   Yes, he *is* very nice . . . Well, I'm late. Good night.

CHUCK   Good night. (*To the audience*) I really didn't expect her to go anyway.

FRAN   What time does the game begin?

CHUCK   Six-thirty. But it's a double header. We don't have to see the first game. We don't even have to see the whole second game. I mean we could come in at the half or the last quarter. All the action's in the last twelve minutes anyway—

FRAN I could meet you at the entrance about nine.

CHUCK Nine! Nine is the perfect time. You don't run into all those early rushers who want to see everything—

FRAN Okay. Then I'll see you at nine.

CHUCK (*He calls after her*) Hey! The *new* Madison Square Garden. The old one is torn down. . . . How about that. She likes basketball! (*He sings*)

She likes basketball, how about that?
We've got something in common to talk about . . .
Basketball.
She likes basketball, how about that?

I have someplace to take her
When we go out . . .
Basketball.
Who ever would have dreamed

Ever would have thought
That my favorite girl liked my favorite sport
Like any other kid I would make believe
With a ball in my hand.

I'd dribble right past
All the others real fast
And I'd be six-foot-eight
And my jump-shot was really great.

She likes basketball, isn't that wild?
It's an omen that good things are on their way.
Things to share . . .

We share basketball, couldn't you die?
From a simple beginning like this
We may get somewhere.

It's nice to dream
Someday it might be
Basketball and me.

Who ever would have dreamed
Ever would have thought
That my favorite girl
Liked my favorite sport.

Like any other kid
I would make believe
With a ball in my hand
I'd dribble right past

All the others real fast
And I'd be six-foot-eight
And my jump-shot was really great.

She likes basketball!
Isn't that wild?
It's an omen that good things
Are on their way
Things to share . . .

We share basketball
Couldn't you die?
From a simple beginning like this
We may get somewhere.

It's nice to dream
Someday it might be
Basketball and me.

Fade Out

SCENE 6

Lum Ding's Chinese Restaurant. There are a number of booths and a couple of scattered tables. The place is a little less than half filled. A lone man sits at the corner table.

The HOSTESS enters and crosses to the exit at the other side. The WAITER then enters and crosses to the exit at the other side. FRAN enters and without looking around heads straight for the lone man at the corner table.

SHELDRAKE Fran . . . Fran, how've you been?

FRAN Fine, Mr. Sheldrake.

SHELDRAKE Mr. Sheldrake? Whatever happened to Jeff?

FRAN Yeah, whatever happened to him?

SHELDRAKE Let me take your coat.

FRAN I can't stay long.

HOSTESS Good evening, miss. (*Points to her head*) You changed your hair. Very pretty.

FRAN Thanks.

SHELDRAKE That's right. You have changed your hair.

FRAN I knew you'd be the first to notice.

SHELDRAKE　Okay, I haven't called you in six weeks. I deserve a little hostility. Am I going to get the egg rolls in the face?

FRAN　I'm waiting for the sauce.

SHELDRAKE　Fran, I missed you.

FRAN　And there it is.

SHELDRAKE　I was going to call you one night last week. I started dialing your number, then hung up in the middle.

FRAN　It must have been Tuesday, the phone didn't ring all night. Can I have a cigarette?

SHELDRAKE　(*He looks at her, then takes out a pack*) First time I ever saw you smoke.

FRAN　I was saving it as a surprise. It's my new image. Joan Crawford, older but wiser.

SHELDRAKE　(*He smiles*) It needs work. You've got the filter at the wrong end.

FRAN　Yeah, well, in case you haven't noticed, I'm nervous as hell about seeing you again.

SHELDRAKE　(*Lighting her cigarette*) I've noticed. I like it. You look great, Fran.

FRAN　Thank you . . . How's the family?

SHELDRAKE　You don't want to hear nice things from me, do you?

FRAN   Yeah, I think it's terrific. You do it better than anyone I know. What'd you have in mind?

SHELDRAKE   You know I haven't worked all day just thinking about you?

FRAN (*She puts her cigarette out, looking down without emotion*)   Well, it's always a little slow before Christmas—

SHELDRAKE (*He grabs her wrist*)   Damn it, Fran, look at me.

FRAN (*She snaps back quickly*)   How do you want me to react, with a chill and a quiver? . . . I did that all summer. And the phone still didn't ring Tuesday night.

SHELDRAKE   Fran, you know neither one of us wanted it to go this far . . . That first night we did nothing but sit here and talk until two in the morning . . .

FRAN   Yeah, just a couple of innocent kids.

SHELDRAKE   What is there about you that makes everything I say so damned phony?

FRAN (*She shrugs*)   Everything you say. Hey, no kidding, Mr. Sheldrake, why did you call me? What do you want?

SHELDRAKE   To look at you . . . to talk to you . . . to see if I can get things started again.

FRAN   Well, that's honest enough . . . Sorry. Next summer I'm going to camp.

SHELDRAKE   It's only November, maybe I can talk you

out of it. Fran, I want you back. I don't want to go another day without seeing you.

FRAN   You've already arranged that. Hostess in the Executive Dining Room. I've gone from "I love you, Fran" to "How are the scallops today?" in two short months.

SHELDRAKE   If you really believe that, Fran, get up and walk out that door right now. I swear, I'll never bother you again . . . Otherwise, sit there and be quiet and listen to me. Because I have something to tell you.

FRAN (*Shrugs*)   Go ahead and tell me. I'm just smoking and drinking.

SHELDRAKE   Damnit, I can't talk here. Can't we go someplace?

FRAN   No. I have a date at nine.

SHELDRAKE   Oh? Important?

FRAN   Not very. But I'm going anyway.
        (*The* WAITER *approaches.* FRAN *takes out a compact and fixes her face*)

WAITER   You like to order dinner now?

FRAN   No. No dinner.

SHELDRAKE   Bring us two more drinks.

FRAN   No more drinks either.

WAITER   Very good. That's no dinner and no more drinks.
        (*He leaves.* FRAN *fixes her hair in the compact's mirror*)

SHELDRAKE I see you still use my birthday present.

FRAN Don't I get to keep it?

SHELDRAKE (*Smiles*) You've got that same petulant look on your face. You had it that first night in Atlantic City.

FRAN Stop it, Jeff . . . Hey, could I have another cigarette? I don't know what to do with my hands.

SHELDRAKE (*Getting up*) I'll get a pack. I have to make a call anyway.

FRAN Do you need change? It's twenty cents to White Plains. (SHELDRAKE *looks at her. There's no point in answering that. He walks off.* FRAN *sits there alone. She picks the compact up from the table and looks at herself*) You know what you would do now if you were smart, don't you? (*She sings "Knowing When to Leave"*)

> Go while the going is good
> Knowing when to leave
> May be the smartest thing
> That anyone can learn.
> Go—
> I'm afraid my heart
> Isn't very smart

> Fly while you still have your wings.
> Knowing when to leave
> Won't ever let you reach
> The point of no return.
> Fly—foolish as it seems
> I still have my dreams

> So I keep hoping, day after day,
> As I wait for the man I need

Night after night
As I wish for a love that can be
Though I'm sure that
No one can tell
Where their wishes and hopes will lead
Somehow I feel
There is happiness just waiting there for me.

When someone walks in your life
You just better be sure he's right
'Cause if he's wrong
There are heartaches and tears you must pay.
Keep both of your eyes on the door
Never let it get out of sight
Just be prepared
When the time has come for you to run away.
Sail when the wind starts to blow.
But like a fool I don't know when to leave . . .

> (*The lights fade on* FRAN *and the Chinese restaurant, although the set stays on. As the lights go up on the right we see* CHUCK *waiting under a sign that says "The New Madison Square Garden"*)

CHUCK (*Looks at his watch*) She's probably having trouble getting crosstown . . . Gee, it must be rough on her trying to get rid of this other fella . . . In a way I feel sorry for the poor guy . . . (*He goes behind a poster looking for her again. The lights go up on* FRAN *as she sings*)

> . . . So I keep hoping day after day
> As I wait for the man I need
> Night after night
> As I wish for a love that can be
> Though I'm sure that
> No one can tell

Norman Shelly as MR. KIRKEBY
Paul Reed as MR. DOBITCH
Vince O'Brien as MR. EICHELBERGER
Dick O'Neill as JESSE VANDERHOF

Where their wishes and hopes will lead
Somehow I feel
There is happiness just waiting there for me.

When someone walks in your life
You just better be sure he's right
'Cause if he's wrong
There are heartaches and tears you must pay.
Keep both of your eyes on the door
Never let it get out of sight
Just be prepared
When the time has come for you to run away.

Sail when the wind starts to blow.
But like a fool I don't know
When to leave—when to leave—when to leave
When to leave.

(*The lights go up on* CHUCK)

CHUCK   Maybe I rushed her? Do you think I moved in too fast? I mean she's just a simple girl, doesn't get around much. Mostly watches basketball at home with her brother . . . Maybe a fast-talking rising young executive like me frightened her . . . Sure . . . That's it . . . (*Looks at his watch*) That's why it's ten-to-eleven . . .
(*The lights go up on* SHELDRAKE *and* FRAN)

SHELDRAKE   (*Returning from his call*) Tommy's got a cold . . . nothing serious.

FRAN   Good. I'm glad everything's all right at home.

SHELDRAKE   You know it isn't, Fran. And it hasn't been for a long time. Remember what we talked about? My getting a divorce?

FRAN   We didn't talk about it, Jeff. You did.

SHELDRAKE I called my lawyer this morning. I'm going through with it, Fran.

FRAN Jeff, let's get something straight. I never asked you to leave your wife.

SHELDRAKE It's my decision. It's what I want.

FRAN Are you sure?

SHELDRAKE I'm sure. If you'll just tell me you still love me.

FRAN You know I do.

SHELDRAKE (*Smiles*) I never doubted it for a minute. Come on.

FRAN Wait a minute. I had a date.

SHELDRAKE You said yourself it wasn't important. (*He kisses her*) Come on.
    (*They exit. The lights go up on* CHUCK)

CHUCK Maybe she caught my cold. Sure, I bet she's in bed as I'm standing here. So I guess I'll get the papers and go home. After all, I'm sure she tried. (*A* WATCHMAN *comes out and locks the door*) Who won?

WATCHMAN Knicks lost one hundred twenty-nine to one hundred twenty-eight in double overtime . . .

CHUCK Well, doesn't sound like we missed much . . .

Blackout

SCENE 7

A single telephone in the lobby of Consolidated Life.
KIRKEBY *is on the phone talking in hushed tones while*
DOBITCH *paces nervously.* VANDERHOF *and* EICHELBERGER
join them.

VANDERHOF Any luck with the kid?

DOBITCH He won't budge. No key, no apartment, no
nothing. And the louse still has a box of my cheese
crackers.

VANDERHOF That rotten kid is using his apartment for
his own selfish needs.

EICHELBERGER Oh, my God, no apartment! What'll we
do?

DOBITCH Will you stop panicking, you dirty old man.

VANDERHOF I'd use my car but the nurse is five-foot-ten
and it's a Volkswagen.
　　　(KIRKEBY *comes out of the booth*)

KIRKEBY Forget it. I just spoke to Hertz and they don't
rent trailers for the night.

VANDERHOF Listen, I have a friend who has a liquor
store with a cot in the back. We can have it Sundays and
Election Day.

EICHELBERGER   But tonight was supposed to be my night.
What am I going to do?

DOBITCH   Why don't you take some hot Ovaltine and go
to bed?

KIRKEBY   It serves us right. Never trust an ambitious kid
with a one-bedroom apartment.

EICHELBERGER   There must be somewhere, someplace—
        (*The music to "Where Can You Take a Girl?"
        begins*)

DOBITCH   Where? Where? (*He sings*)

    Where can you if you're a man
    Take a girl if she's a girl
    That you can't
    Can't ever take home for a little drink
    Like other guys who live alone can do?
    That is the reason why
    Most married men are true.

    Aside from hotels
    Where can you on Tuesday night
    Take a girl who's out of sight
    That you can't
    Can't ever take home for a little fun
    Chase her around the room until you win?
    That is the reason why
    Most single men stay thin.

    Aside from motels
    Where can you if you're alone
    Take a girl who's on her own
    That you can't

Can't ever take home on your one night out
One night to be a man and not a mouse?
Most married men play cards
Most single men play house
We'd like to play house too.

All we need is one place
A small apartment, a truck or trailer, old or new
Oh there must be some place
A baby carriage, a kiddy car will do
We aren't proud.
Where can you take a girl that you just
Can't take home?

(*The set changes to the Executive Dining Room*)
You know, if it were a little warmer I'd even take Sylvia
to Central Park.

VANDERHOF   And take a chance of being mugged?

DOBITCH   Nahh, she's a very nice girl. (*Singing*)

Where can you if you are free
Take a girl you'd like to see
That you can't
Can't ever take home on a weekday night
Put on some records and then go berserk?
Most single men we know
Work hardest after work.

Aside from rowboats
Where can you, a man that's true
Take a girl who gets to you
That you can't can't ever take home for a little whirl
Dance her around so fast she starts to shout?
Most married men just waltz
Most single men make out
We'd like to make out too.

All we need is one place
For sixty minutes or forty minutes more or less
Oh there must be some place
In twenty minutes we'll find happiness
We can be fast
In fact we always are.

Aside from rooftops
Where can you if you are free
Take a girl you'd like to see
That you can't ever take home?
What's there left to do
But to go home to
Our wives!

> (*At the conclusion of the number,* CHUCK *enters the room gaily. He is dressed a lot better now that he is a Junior Executive. He crosses to his "usual" table near the window, sits and looks at the menu. He nods at the "boys" and gives them a little wave with his fingers, then looks back at the menu. They mumble obscenities under their breath*)

Look at him, calm, well-rested, the little fink.

> (FRAN *enters from the kitchen, wearing a pert hostess uniform. She carries a glass of sherry on a serving dish. She crosses to* CHUCK)

FRAN   Good afternoon, Mr. Baxter.
(*She puts down the drink*)

CHUCK   Oh, hello.

FRAN   A dry sherry before lunch, isn't it?

CHUCK   Yes. You have a wonderful memory.

FRAN   Not for some things.

CHUCK   Oh, you mean the basketball game? I've forgotten about that. I told you yesterday.

FRAN   You didn't wait outside all night, did you?

CHUCK   No . . . just about fifteen minutes, then I went in. It was a terrific game.

FRAN   I had no excuse.

CHUCK   Well, that's plenty good enough for me. After all, I'm sure you couldn't help yourself . . . How's the chicken pot pie?

FRAN   You shouldn't be so understanding. I'm not worth it.

CHUCK   Miss Kubelik, one doesn't get to be a Junior Second Administrative Assistant around here unless he's a pretty good judge of character . . . and as far as I'm concerned, you're tops. I mean decency-wise and otherwise-wise.

FRAN   Will that be all?

CHUCK   That'll be all . . . unless you're not busy Thursday night? I'm usually free on Thursdays.

FRAN   I'm usually not.

CHUCK   (*Smiles*)   Then I guess that'll be all. (*To the audience*) Cheers. (*The* FOUR EXECS *approach*) I know. I see them.
    (FRAN *nods and exits into the kitchen as the* FOUR EXECS *surround* CHUCK *at his table*)

DOBITCH   Dry sherry dry enough for you, kid?

VANDERHOF   Nice big table all for yourself.

KIRKEBY   Hot food, warm plates, clean silverware.

EICHELBERGER   This is the life, heh, Chuck, boy?

CHUCK (*Smiles*)   Well, I'm not without contentment, no.
  (*He sips his sherry*)

DOBITCH   You've got it all now, Baxter. Success . . . accomplishment . . . security . . .

VANDERHOF   But there's one thing missing, kid.

CHUCK   What's that?

KIRKEBY   Gratitude. We don't see any gratitude, do we, boys?
  (*They all shake their heads "no"*)

CHUCK   Well, I certainly don't want to seem ungrateful . . . How about four chicken pot pies?
  (*They gather around him*)

VANDERHOF   Don't play with us, kid. Don't toy with angry middle-aged executives.

CHUCK   Look, fellas, for your information, my apartment is private property, not a public playground. I don't understand what happens to men when they get to be your age.

DOBITCH   Don't understand us. Help us!
     (*The* FOUR EXECS *sing*)

All we need is one place
For sixty minutes or forty minutes
More or less
Oh, there must be some place
In twenty minutes we'll find happiness
We can be fast
Where can you take a girl
That you just can't take home

     (*They exit, singing*)

Where can you, if you're a man
Take a girl, if she's a girl . . .

     (*The lights black out, leaving a spot on* CHUCK,
     who steps out front to the audience)

CHUCK   In a way I sympathized with them. As middle-
aged men they wanted to have occasionally what they
thought young men like me have regularly. But I wasn't
having it regularly. As a matter of fact, I wasn't even
having what they have occasionally . . . it's something
for you to think about. (*He crosses to* SHELDRAKE, *who is
reclining on a sun deck chaise*) Oh, Mr. Sheldrake
. . . they told me I'd find you here on the Executive
Sun Deck.

SHELDRAKE   Am I getting too red?

CHUCK   Not for me, J.D. You have the kind of skin
that bronzes nicely.

SHELDRAKE   You've got your promotion. Don't butter me.
I like you, Baxter, but let's understand each other. We

may have a reciprocal arrangement that fulfills certain mutual needs, but in no way does it mean we're bosom buddies. I'm starting you on the very lowest rung of the executive ladder but you'll have to climb upward on your own initiative. I may have a private life to lead but I also have a department to run.

CHUCK Well, may I say you lead them and run them beautifully, sir. I just dropped up because I have something here I think belongs to you.
(*He reaches in his pocket*)

SHELDRAKE (*Puts down his reflector*) To me?

CHUCK I mean the young lady, whoever she may be. It was on the couch when I got home last night. It's a compact. (*He takes out* FRAN's *gold compact*) I'm afraid the mirror is broken.

SHELDRAKE I know. She threw it at me. Fortunately I ducked. Was there any damage?
(*He takes the compact*)

CHUCK Oh, nothing much. A little hole in an old Van Gogh print on the wall. Luckily it went right through the sunset. (*Reaches in his pocket*) I have all the broken pieces of the mirror in my pocket if you care to put them together . . .

SHELDRAKE You know, Baxter, I envy you.

CHUCK Me? Why?

SHELDRAKE Your life is simple. A bachelor who can have

an affair with no complications, no promises made that you can't possibly keep. You've got it made, right?

CHUCK If you say so, sir. (*He turns to the audience*) Why is it everyone envies me except me?
>   (CHUCK *exits.* SHELDRAKE *turns and looks out over the sun deck, then takes* FRAN's *mirror out of his pocket and looks at it. He sings "Wanting Things"*)

Tell me how long must I keep wanting things
Needing things, when I have so much?
There are many men who have much less than me
Day by day they make their way
And they find more in life than I can see.
Tell me

When will I learn to resist wanting things
Touching things that say
Do, do not touch.
People that I meet seem to think I am strong
They don't see inside of me
So they don't know I'm weak and often wrong.

Tell me why must I keep wanting things
Needing things that just can't be mine.
Oh wanting things that just can't be
Mine.

(*He exits*)

Blackout

Scene 8

Outside the elevator. FRAN *appears and looks around.* MISS OLSON *comes out of an elevator, somewhat tipsy, holding a paper cup full of liquor.*

FRAN Excuse me, can you tell me where the Christmas party is?

MISS OLSON (*Points up*) One floor down.

FRAN (*Smiles*) Thank you.
(*She starts to walk away*)

MISS OLSON Hey, aren't you the branch manager from Kansas City?

FRAN I beg your pardon.

MISS OLSON I'm Miss Olson, Mr. Sheldrake's secretary.

FRAN Yes, I know.

MISS OLSON Four years ago I was the branch manager from Minneapolis.

FRAN I'm sorry, I don't understand—

MISS OLSON I know what you're going through, honey. I got the same routine, from a weekend in Atlantic City right through to Chinese food.

FRAN I'm afraid I don't know what you're talking about.
(*She starts to turn away*)

MISS OLSON Oh, come on, sugar, I know all about it. I'm very perceptive . . . and I also listen in on his telephone calls. (*She rocks a bit*) . . . You know I never drank before I met Jeff. I smoke now too . . . and I put on twelve pounds . . . Which is why I now smoke and drink and you're the new branch manager from Kansas City.

FRAN Miss Olson, if you'll excuse me . . .

MISS OLSON It's all right, honey, you're in good company. He only picks the cutest girls. Miss Rossi in Auditing, Miss Koch in Disability, Miss Della Hoya from Petty Cash—we thought we'd meet once a year for lunch at Schrafft's. When we get two more girls we're going to charter a boat ride to Bear Mountain.

FRAN Miss Olson, I don't know what you've heard, but I can assure you—

MISS OLSON What a salesman. If our affair lasted two more days I would have bought insurance from him. But you'll buy it too, sweetie. The same pitch about divorcing his wife, only by the time the papers come through, you'll be telling some cute receptionist what I'm telling you . . .
(*She raises her hand*)

FRAN I'm sure you mean well, Miss Olson—

MISS OLSON (*Shrugs*) Some people give to the Heart Fund, I warn girls about Sheldrake . . . You want to be smart, honey? Take the compact he bought you that I picked out, trade it in for a pair of track shoes and run for your life. (*Looks in her cup*) Excuse me, my stupor is wearing off. I've got to re-stupe.

Blackout

Scene 9

The nineteenth floor. The floor is decked out in Christmas trimming, the desks are all pushed together for "Turkey Lurkey." DOBITCH *stands on a desk.*

DOBITCH   And now, ladies and gentlemen, the Christmas Party Committee has asked the Idea Committee to come up with an idea for the Christmas Party. So without further ado, I give you Miss Polansky of Accounts Receivable, Miss Wong of Mimeograph, and Miss Della Hoya of Petty Cash.
   (*They sing*)

It's Turkey Lurkey time
Tom Turkey ran away but he just came home.
It's Turkey Lurkey time
He's really come to stay never more to roam.
Let us make a wish
And may all your wishes come true.
A snowy blowy Christmas
A mistletoey Christmas
A Turkey Lurkey Christmas to you
A Turkey Lurkey Christmas to you.

It's Goosey Poosey time
She was a gadabout but she's back again.
It's Goosey Poosey time
Her time is running out and we all know when.
Let us make a wish
And may all your wishes come true.

A snowy blowy Christmas
A mistletoey Christmas
A Goosey Poosey Christmas to you
A Goosey Poosey Christmas to you.

Turkey Lurkey
Goosey Poosey
Some for Uncle Joe
And some for Cousin Lucy.
Everybody gather round the table
Dig in, dinner's being served
Eat all the turkey you are able
If you see a partridge in a pear tree
Climb up and bring it down for me
That's something I would like to see.

> (*They dance a wild dance, urged on, and later
> joined by, all the employees. When the dance is
> over the girls again sing*)

A snowy blowy Christmas
A mistletoey Christmas
A Turkey Lurkey Christmas
To you-ou-ou.

Jingle Bells, Jingle Bells,
Jingle Bells, Jingle Bells,
Merry Christmas,
Merry Christmas.

DOBITCH   Listen, kid, did you get my note? I meant what
I said. The keys to my Jaguar and my Diners Club card
for the entire Christmas holidays.

CHUCK   Yeah, sure, Mr. Dobitch, anything you want.
You just caught me at the right season.

DOBITCH   Good. You leave the keys under the doormat. I'll be there at four o'clock.

CHUCK   Hey, you didn't see Miss Kubelik around here, did you? (*She appears on the opposite side of the stage*) Never mind, I just felt her presence. (*He crosses to* FRAN, *who is glum*) Hi. Glad you could make it up to the nineteenth floor. I hear the eighteenth floor's already been arrested. (*He laughs*) Can I get you a drink?

FRAN (*Downhearted*)   No thanks.

CHUCK   Is anything wrong?

FRAN   No, there are just too many people here.

CHUCK   Funny how we're beginning to think alike. (*Takes her arm*) Miss Kubelik, I would like to show you something. (*They cross to the desk, where a couple is necking*) Ahem. (*The couple exits quickly*) Boy, are they drunk. Those two are married to each other. (*He takes a box from the desk drawer*) Miss Kubelik, I want your honest opinion. I've had this in my desk for a week. (*He shows her the hat*) Cost me twenty-three bucks, but I just couldn't get the nerve up to wear it. (*Puts on a gray homburg*) It's called "Young Exec" . . . comes with a free subscription to the *Wall Street Journal* . . . Remember, an honest opinion. (*He poses; she looks dumbly*) All right, I'll accept a dishonest opinion . . . You hate it. I look like Sidney Greenstreet in "The Maltese Falcon" . . . I agree. Well, there's a doctor in my building I owe a Christmas present . . .

FRAN   No, I like it. Very distinguished.

CHUCK Really? Classy Distinguished or Trying Distinguished? I mean I don't want to get an Al Capone effect.

FRAN I like the way you look. I really do.

CHUCK How about that? Listen, maybe I'll try it out this afternoon on Fifth Avenue. I sure could use some moral support.

FRAN Oh . . . This is a bad day for me.

CHUCK I understand. Christmas, family and all that . . .

FRAN Well, I'd better get back to the Dining Room. They must be wondering where I am.

CHUCK Hey, you sure you like the hat? I mean, is the angle good for my face?

FRAN I think so. Here, look for yourself.
  (*She takes out her compact and gives it to him*)

CHUCK After all, this is a conservative firm. I wouldn't want people to think I was a ward heeler or something . . .
  (*As he looks in the compact mirror his voice gives out.* FRAN *notices his peculiar expression*)

FRAN What's wrong?

CHUCK The mirror . . . it's broken.

FRAN I know. I like it this way . . . makes me look the way I feel. (*The phone rings.* CHUCK *doesn't hear it.*

He closes the compact, hands it back to FRAN) . . . Your phone.

CHUCK Oh. (*He picks up the phone*) Yes? (*Throws a quick look at* FRAN) Just a minute. (*He covers the phone with his hand and speaks to* FRAN) If you don't mind, this is sort of personal.

FRAN All right. Have a nice Christmas.
    (CHUCK *nods. She exits.* CHUCK *takes his hand off the mouthpiece*)

CHUCK (*Every word hurts*) Yes, Mr. Sheldrake . . . No, I didn't forget . . . the tree is up and the Tom and Jerry mix is in the refrigerator . . . Yes, sir, the same to you.
    (*He hangs up and stands there for a moment, the new hat still on his head. He sits on the desk chair*)

Curtain

Act Two

Scene 1

CHUCK *is sitting at a booth in Clancy's Lounge, a seedy Eighth Avenue bar. He looks up at the audience, obviously drunk.*

CHUCK   I'd rather not talk about it if you don't mind . . . Just look at me . . . in some seedy bar . . . God knows where . . . cheaping up slop whiskey . . . slopping up cheap whiskey . . . I disgust me . . . I mean what did I expect? That she was some kind of pure, untouched, unblemished rose just waiting for me to come along? . . . Yes, that's what I expected . . . Listen, I don't want to talk to you any more . . . I'll call you next week . . . (*He crosses to the bar and* BARTENDER EUGENE. *He puts money on the bar*) Eugene, Eugene, I'd like twenty-two dollars' worth of cheering up.

> (BARTENDER EUGENE *pours him a shot.* MARGE *crosses to* CHUCK *with her empty glass*)

MARGE (*Warm smile*)   Hello, there. All alone I see.

CHUCK (*He looks at* MARGE, *then at the audience*)   I think I'm gonna be all right. (*To* MARGE) Hello there yourself.

MARGE   As it happens, I'm alone too.

CHUCK   As what happens?

MARGE   Ooh, fast with the repartee, aren't you? In

point of fact, I'm just trying to be friendly. I mean the world is hostile enough, isn't it?

CHUCK   Everywhere you turn.

MARGE   And your name is?—

CHUCK   (*Lifts his hat*) Baxter. C. C. Baxter.
(*He drops the hat back on his head*)

MARGE   Ohh, initials. That's very fancy . . . I'm just plain Margie MacDougall.

CHUCK   (*Looks her up and down*)   I don't see anything plain about you, Margie.

MARGE   Oh, touché! . . . (*She looks at her empty glass*) My goodness, have I finished that stinger already?

CHUCK   (*To* BARTENDER EUGENE)   Eugene, another stinger. Here.

MARGE   Oh, isn't that sweet? That really isn't necessary. (*Quickly to* BARTENDER EUGENE) Double on the vodka, Eugene. (*To* CHUCK) By the by, before we go any further, I wouldn't want you to get the wrong idea about me. I'm *not* a pickup.

CHUCK   Never crossed my mind.

MARGE   Sociable maybe, but not a pickup . . . I'm just looking for a drink and some friendly conversation, that's all.

CHUCK   Got you, Marge.

MARGE I mean I have no intention of going *any*where with *any*one for *any*thing.

CHUCK Good girl, Marge.

MARGE Why, do you have a place near here? . . . That's conversation, not curiosity. As I said, I'm not a pickup.

CHUCK Anyone could tell from the way you dress . . . Très chic.

MARGE (*Flattered*) Oh, gracias . . . You like this coat? It's owl. I actually swear on my mother's life, it's made from those birds with the big eyes that see in the dark and go "Hoo." A gift from my late husband, Jerome.

CHUCK Oh, a widow.

MARGE (*Takes a drink*) Well, I'm not dead certain I'm a widow, but when you don't hear from your husband in twenty-two months there's no point in keeping the roast warm. Sköl!
  (*She drinks her vodka stinger*)

CHUCK Two years is a long time to be lonely.

MARGE I don't recall saying I was lonely. Have I indicated to you in any way whatever that I was lonely? Indeed not. So don't be getting any fancy ideas in that rather attractive head of yours.

CHUCK So you find me attractive, eh, Marge?

MARGE You catch everything, don't you . . . I don't mean to imply attractive in any sexual way. Nor do I wish to imply that you are *un*attractive in a sexual way

. . . What I *do* want to imply is that I'm not thinking in a sexual way at all. Not to imply that I've *never* thought in a sexual way. But I am, technically speaking, still in a state of mourning. So can we just drop the subject of sex, Mr. Fast-on-your-feet?

CHUCK   How's your stinger?

MARGE   You *are* persuasive, aren't you? (*She hands her glass to* BARTENDER EUGENE *for a refill*) Question. You married?

CHUCK   Answer. No!

MARGE   Family?

CHUCK   In Ohio.

MARGE   Mm. A night like this, Christmas Eve and all, it's not much fun walking into an empty apartment, is it?

CHUCK   I said I wasn't married. I didn't say I had an empty apartment.

MARGE   It wouldn't make any difference because I have no intention of going there, as I previously indicated . . . So just get it right out of your mind, Mr. C. C. Baxter with the sweet-smelling after-shave cologne that just happens to be my favorite.

CHUCK   You like Aqua Velva?

MARGE   Oh, yes. Jerome used it by the gallon. He was quite masculine, you know. Used to shave three, four times a day.

Jerry Orhbach as CHUCK BAXTER
Jill O'Hara as FRAN KUBELIK
A. Larry Haines as DR. DREYFUSS

CHUCK Boy . . . They don't make 'em like that any more.

MARGE I didn't mean to imply that you're *not* masculine. In your own off-beat way, I suppose you are. I mean with the light behind you and your chapeau at that jaunty angle, you remind me somewhat of Jerome, if I remember him correctly.

CHUCK —But Jerome isn't here.

MARGE (*She nods in agreement*) But Jerome isn't here.

CHUCK And "rather attractive" me is.

MARGE (*Nods*) And rather attractive you is.

CHUCK Those are facts we've got to face, Marge.

MARGE Well, you're definitely a fact . . . (*She sings*)
  And a fact can be a beautiful thing
  When the fact I am facing is you.

CHUCK (*Singing*)
  A fact can be a terrible thing
  When the dreams you've been dreaming fall through.

CHUCK *and* MARGE
  Forget the past and think about the present
  Right now is everything.
  Forget the past and think about the present,

CHUCK
  The present's very pleasant.

CHUCK *and* MARGE

Who cares what the future will bring?
There's just no predicting a thing.
Don't wait for a miracle
Because it's Christmas
Not a time to be alone with memories.
Christmas is supposed to be a happy holiday
Throw a little joy my way,

MARGE

You could really make my day,

CHUCK

Throw a little joy my way,

MARGE

And a fact can be a beautiful thing
When I can see what I'm seeing in you.

CHUCK

A fact can be a wonderful thing
When your hopes to be happy come true.

CHUCK *and* MARGE

What's gone is gone and don't you ever doubt it,
Wake up and start to live.
What's gone is gone so learn to live without it

CHUCK

And never think about it.

CHUCK AND MARGE

Who cares what the future will bring?
There's just no predicting a thing.
Don't wait for a miracle
Because it's Christmas

Not a time to be alone with memories.
Christmas is supposed to be a happy holiday
Throw a little joy my way.

MARGE

Do we really have to stay?

CHUCK

Throw a little joy my way . . .

(*They start out, but are stopped by the singing of the* PATRONS *and employees, who insist on having a drink with them*)

ALL

Forget the past and think about the present
Right now is everything.
Forget the past and think about the present,
The present's very pleasant.
Who cares what the future will bring?
There's just no predicting a thing.
Don't wait for a miracle
Because it's Christmas
Not the time to be alone with memories.
Christmas
Is supposed to be a happy holiday
Throw a little joy my way.

(*An accidental rhythm occurs, caused by noises of a tray, two whiskey bottles, a laugh.* CHUCK *improvises a dance step to the rhythm. The others join in, till all are dancing the Game, including a first-reluctant* MARGE)

Because it's Christmas
Just the perfect night
For us to dance and sing.

Christmas
Is supposed to be a happy holiday
Happy holiday
So throw a little joy my way.

(CHUCK *and* MARGE *exit. The* PATRONS *dance in
couples and sing*)

Forget the past and think about the present
Right now is everything.
Forget the past and think about the present,
The present's very pleasant.
Who cares what the future will bring?
There's just no predicting a thing . . .

Blackout

CHUCK's *apartment. The living room is dark, except for a shaft of light from the kitchen, and the glow of the colored bulbs on a small Christmas tree in front of the phony fireplace.*

Hunched up in one corner of the couch is FRAN, *still in her coat and gloves, crying softly. Pacing up and down is* SHELDRAKE. *His coat and hat are on the chair, as are several Christmas packages. On the coffee table are an unopened bottle of Scotch, a couple of untouched glasses and a bowl of melting ice.*

SHELDRAKE (*Looking very upset as* FRAN *cries*) Come on, Fran, don't be like that. You just going to sit there, crying? (*No answer. He tries a new approach*) Look, I know you think I'm stalling you. But when you've been married to a woman for twelve years, you don't just sit down at the breakfast table and say, "Helen, can I please have the sugar and a divorce." (*He resumes pacing,* FRAN *keeps sobbing*) Anyway, this is the wrong time. The kids are home from school, the in-laws are visiting for the holidays. I can't bring it up *now*. (*Stops*) For God's sake, Fran, are you going to listen to me or are you going to keep crying?

FRAN (*Sobs*) I can do both.

SHELDRAKE You know, this isn't like you, Fran. You were always such a good sport, such fun to be with.

FRAN   That's me, the Happy Idiot. Short on brains but a million laughs.

SHELDRAKE   I didn't mean it that way . . .

FRAN   It's true. I laugh easily. I even got a big chuckle today out of your secretary, Miss Olson. You remember her, the branch manager from Minneapolis?

SHELDRAKE   Is that what's bothering you? Miss Olson? For God's sakes, Fran, that's ancient history.

FRAN   Well, she brought me up with more current events . . . like Miss Koch, Miss Rossi, Miss Della Hoya . . . How do you work it, Jeff, alphabetical order or one floor at a time?

SHELDRAKE   Oh, come on, Fran . . .

FRAN   It must have been rough when they switched to automatic elevators. All those cute little operators going to waste—

SHELDRAKE   All right, Fran, I suppose I deserved that.

FRAN   Try *definitely*.

SHELDRAKE   Damnit, don't you understand that no one —*no one* means anything to me any more except you? Fran, I don't like to see you like this.

FRAN   (*She takes a handkerchief from her purse*)   Did I tell you I'm writing a book? *Affairs Can Be Fun*. (*Wipes her eyes*) Chapter One, Never Wear Mascara When You're in Love with a Married Man.

SHELDRAKE It's Christmas Eve, Fran. Let's not fight.

FRAN Merry Christmas.
(*She throws a package to him*)

SHELDRAKE What is it?

FRAN A scarf. I knitted it the six nights a week I don't see you.

SHELDRAKE Fran, if it were possible I would *never* leave . . .

FRAN (*She takes out a small leather frame from her purse*) And I had that picture we took on the boardwalk framed. I bought it as a gift from you to me. I know you don't have much time to do any shopping . . .

SHELDRAKE As a matter of fact, I wanted to get you something . . . But you never know who you run into in department stores . . . (*He takes out a money clip, detaches a bill*) . . . so here's a hundred dollars . . . go out and buy yourself something. (*He holds the money out but she doesn't move.* SHELDRAKE *slips the bill into her open bag*) . . . They have some nice alligator bags at Bergdorf's . . . (FRAN *gets up and slowly starts peeling off her gloves.* SHELDRAKE *looks at her, then nervously glances at his watch*) . . . Fran, it's a quarter to seven— and I mustn't miss the train tonight—if we hadn't wasted all that time—well, I have to get home and trim the tree . . .

FRAN (*Having started to remove her coat*) Oh. Okay. (*She shrugs, puts her coat back on*) I just thought as long as it was paid for—

SHELDRAKE (*He takes an angry step toward her*) Don't ever talk like that, Fran. Don't make yourself out to be cheap.

FRAN   A hundred dollars? I wouldn't call that cheap. And you must be paying someone for the use of the apartment—

SHELDRAKE   Fran, the last thing I want to do is to hurt you.

FRAN (*She stares at him*) You'll miss your train, Jeff.
(SHELDRAKE *releases her, then hurriedly puts on his hat and coat, and gathers up his packages*)

SHELDRAKE   Are you coming?

FRAN   You run along—I want to fix what's left of my face.

SHELDRAKE (*Nods*) Don't forget to kill the lights . . . I'll see you next week.

FRAN (*With bite*) I have it marked on my calendar. I draw a little heart around all the Thursdays.

SHELDRAKE   It won't always be like this, Fran . . . I love you, you know.

FRAN   I never doubted it for a minute. (*He bends to kiss her; she pulls away*) Careful . . . lipstick.
(*He kisses her cheek, looks at her uncomfortably, and then goes, closing the door behind him. Music begins.* FRAN *crosses back to the sofa and sits a moment, then picks up the photograph she has placed down and looks at it. . . . She sings "Whoever You Are"*)

Sometimes your eyes look blue to me
Although I know they're really green.
I seem to see you differently
Changing as I'm treated kindly
Or treated meanly.
From moment to moment
You're two different people
Faithful and warm when I'm in your arms
And then when you leave, you're so untrue, but
However you are, deep down whatever you are
Whoever you are, I love you.

Sometimes I feel you're mine alone
And yet I'm sure it's just not so.
I get this feeling on my own
After I learn if you're staying
Or if you're going.
From moment to moment
You're two different people
Someone I know as the man I love
Or the man I wish I never knew, but

However you are
Deep down whatever you are
Whoever you are, I love you.

Sometimes your eyes look blue to me.

*(After the song, she suddenly starts to sob, then
crosses to the bed. She takes a Kleenex and starts
wiping off her mascara. Then she notices a vial
of pills on the table. She takes it. Then she sits
back and stares at it. The lights in the apartment
dim and go to black. Outside in the vestibule we
see* CHUCK *and* MARGE)

CHUCK   Just five more steps to Paradise.

MARGE   I still haven't made up my mind if I'm going in there. I mean, can I trust you?

CHUCK   Not for a minute, Marge.

MARGE   Well, I guess a girl can't get hurt in a minute, can she? (*She laughs, then staggers*) Whoops . . . Don't push.

CHUCK   Hey, Marge, are you all right?

MARGE   So they tell me . . . Oh, heavens, you must think I'm awful.

CHUCK (*Grins*)   I think you're peachy.

MARGE   Oh, you're a smooth talker . . . I can see I'm going to have my hands full with you, Mr. Ready-for-Everything.

CHUCK   An apt description, Mrs. MacDougall. (*He opens the door*) Enter. (*Switches on the light*) Like it?

MARGE (*Looks around*)   Well, I'm not looking to rent it. (CHUCK *closes the door*) Just the one room, is it?

CHUCK   And there's a bed back there, in case you were wondering.

MARGE   One more remark like that and I'm going to ask you to leave the door ajar.

CHUCK   May I take your owl?

MARGE   Hoo! Not wasting any time, are you?

CHUCK   Not preliminary-wise. (*He takes her coat off*)

You beginning to get the feeling, Mrs. MacDougall, you are in the clutches of a raving sex-pot?

MARGE   I may as well warn you now, erotic language doesn't arouse me . . . So don't be so sure of yourself.

CHUCK   I'm as cute as the dickens and you know it . . . You are looking at the only male rape victim in this neighborhood.

MARGE   (*Smiles*) That's adorable. You are not totally without charm.

CHUCK   And I haven't started yet. (*He crosses to the phonograph*) Why don't you bat those big blue eyes at the refrigerator and melt some ice, while I put on my theme song.

MARGE   I wish you'd stop being so attractive. I'm beginning to think wicked thoughts.
        (*She gives him a flutter of her eyes and goes into the kitchen.* CHUCK *takes off his hat and tosses it on a chair. He skips to the door and bolts it. He rubs his hands eagerly, then notices* FRAN's *bag on the coffee table. He takes it over to the screened area and tosses it over and onto the bed. He starts away when he realizes what he has just seen. He pushes the screen back revealing* FRAN *in the bed. She is still dressed but appears to be in a deep sleep, almost lifeless.* CHUCK, *annoyed, shakes her*)

CHUCK   All right, Miss Kubelik, get up . . . It's past checkout time and the hotel management would appreciate it if you would check out! *Now!* (FRAN *doesn't stir*) Look, Miss Kubelik, I used to like you. I used to like you a lot— but it's all over between us—so beat it! O-U-T! *Out!* (*No*

reaction. He puts a hand on her shoulder and shakes her more vigorously) Come on, wake up! You wanna sleep, go home! *(She doesn't respond. He notices something in her fist. He opens it and removes the vial which contained the sleeping pills, now empty. He shakes it upside down)* Oh, my God! *(For a second he is paralyzed. Then he drops the vial and grabs* FRAN, *and shakes her violently)* Miss Kubelik!! *Miss Kubelik!! (*FRAN's *head drops to one side like a rag doll.* CHUCK *lets go of her, then dashes into the living room. He rushes to the phone and dials quickly. He speaks into the phone)* Hello, operator, get me the police. *(Thinks about that)* No! . . . No, don't get me the police.
> *(*MARGE *comes out of the kitchen with a bowlful of ice cubes)*

MARGE   Your ice cube tray isn't cooperating at all. You really ought to get a new refrigerator. *(*CHUCK *ignores her and runs out of the apartment)* . . . Hey, I didn't mean *right now!*
> *(She shrugs and goes back into the kitchen.* CHUCK, *in the vestibule, bangs on* DR. DREYFUSS's *door)*

CHUCK   Doctor Dreyfuss! Hey, Doc! *(He bangs on the door)* Come on, please, you've got to be home. *(The door opens and* DR. DREYFUSS *stands there sleepily, pulling on his bathrobe)* There's a girl in my place—she took some sleeping pills—you'd better come quick, I can't wake her up . . .

DR. DREYFUSS   Let me get my bag.
> *(He goes back into his apartment.* CHUCK *turns and goes back into his apartment as* MARGE *comes out of the kitchen holding a bottle)*

MARGE   Look what I found. Tom and Jerries. You sly dog!

CHUCK (*Takes her arm and pulls her*) Come on. Let's go.

MARGE (*Smiling vacantly*) Aren't we rushing things?

CHUCK The party's over. Nothing personal.

MARGE (*Being pushed toward the door*) I don't understand.

CHUCK Come on.

MARGE (*Taking his arm off her*) I'm going to ask you not to get physical.

CHUCK It's an emergency. I'll see you some other Christmas.

MARGE (*Suddenly she hears* FRAN *moan. She looks and sees her*) Who's that? Where did she come from? (DR. DREYFUSS *comes in and looks at* MARGE) Who's he?

CHUCK (*To* DR. DREYFUSS) Not this one, Doc— (*Points to the bed*) The other one!
   (DR. DREYFUSS *rushes in to* FRAN)

MARGE What's going on here? Who are these people?

CHUCK Please!

MARGE Oh, my God! *It's an orgy!*

CHUCK (*To* MARGE) Would you please go! Now!

MARGE An orgy—on Christmas Eve! It's the most disgusting thing I've ever run across.

CHUCK (*He hands her his last few dollars*)   Here! Take a taxi! Get another stinger, only please go!

MARGE (*Takes the money*)   I should have known. The minute I saw you walk in the bar with that dignified hat I knew you were a pervert!

CHUCK   Well, that's the way it is.
   (*He pushes her out in the hall and closes the door. She pulls her coat around her and starts out*)

MARGE   Filthy, filthy perverts! (*She knocks on* DR. DREYFUSS's *closed door and yells in*) They're having an orgy on the second floor! . . . Oh, God, I think I'm going to be sick!
   (*She runs out and disappears.* CHUCK *rushes back to* DR. DREYFUSS *who is examining* FRAN's *eyes with a flashlight*)

CHUCK   Is she gonna be all right, Doc?

DR. DREYFUSS   How many pills were in that bottle?
   (*He takes out a stomach tube from his bag*)

CHUCK   Twelve. I only used one . . . Is that enough— to do it?

DR. DREYFUSS   Without even trying. Help me with her.
   (*They get* FRAN *into an upright position. They half-carry, half-drag* FRAN's *limp form toward the bathroom*)

CHUCK   What are you going to do?

DR. DREYFUSS   Get that stuff out of her stomach, if it isn't too late.
   (*He takes* FRAN *himself*)

CHUCK (*Stepping back*) Oh, God . . . My God . . .

DR. DREYFUSS First put on some hot coffee . . . then you can ask your friend God for His help . . . (CHUCK *backs away as* DR. DREYFUSS *enters the bathroom with the limp* FRAN. *The lights fade. About fifteen minutes later:* DR. DREYFUSS *is placing* FRAN *on the sofa as* CHUCK *stands watching fearfully, the hot coffee pot in his hand*) Get my bag. (CHUCK *quickly gets him his bag, and looks bewildered.* DR. DREYFUSS *has taken out a needle and syringe and measures off the correct amount of c.c.'s from a medical bottle*) First put the coffee down, dummy. (CHUCK *puts down the pot.* DR. DREYFUSS *feels her arm for the right spot to inject*) Nice veins. You've seen them before, I guess.

CHUCK Huh?

DR. DREYFUSS (*He swabs a spot with alcohol and takes the hypodermic needle from* CHUCK) Want to tell me what happened?
(*He injects her arm*)

CHUCK I don't know . . . I wasn't here . . . I mean, we had some words earlier . . . nothing serious . . . what you might call a lovers' spat.

DR. DREYFUSS Some spat. Eleven pills worth.

CHUCK I didn't know she was so upset . . .

DR. DREYFUSS When did you pick up the other tootsie? *Before* she took the pills or *during*?

CHUCK I wouldn't have picked up the other one if I knew she was still here . . .

DR. DREYFUSS You know, Baxter, for a fink you got a lotta class.
> (*He starts to slap* FRAN *in the face. She moans and reacts*)

CHUCK (*Enormous relief*) Look, Doc, she's breathing . . .

DR. DREYFUSS If it annoys you, I can turn it off. (*He takes an ampule out of his bag*) A half hour later you'd have found some Christmas present. (*He breaks it under her nose. She winces*) Give me that coffee. (CHUCK *hands him the pot and mug*) Open those windows. Get some air in here. It smells from disillusionment. (CHUCK *quickly rushes to the windows, pulls up the shades and opens the windows wide.* DR. DREYFUSS *pours coffee into a mug and then tries to get* FRAN *to sip some. She coughs*) What's her name?

CHUCK Fran, Kubelik.
> (*He crosses back to them*)

DR. DREYFUSS Fran, I'm a doctor. I'm here because you took too many sleeping pills. Do you understand what I'm saying? (FRAN *mutters*) Come on, Fran, pay attention.
> (*He slaps her face again. She winces*)

CHUCK (*Winces too*) Doesn't that hurt her, Doc?

DR. DREYFUSS (*Scowling at him*) For deep concern, you got lousy timing. (*To* FRAN) Fran, do you know where you are? . . . Do you know whose apartment this is, Fran?

FRAN (*Sleepily*) No . . .

DR. DREYFUSS (*Pulls* CHUCK *over in front of her*) Do you know who this is, Fran? . . . Look at him!

FRAN (*Looks at him*) Mr. Baxter—

CHUCK Hello, Miss Kubelik.

DR. DREYFUSS Mister—Miss—pretty formal for a suicide.

CHUCK Well, we work for the same company and we try to keep it quiet.

FRAN (*Puzzled, to* CHUCK) What are you doing here?
(CHUCK *looks at* DR. DREYFUSS *as if to say "Her mind still isn't functioning"*)

CHUCK (*To* FRAN) Don't you remember? We were at the office party together?

FRAN The office party—Miss Olson—

CHUCK (*To* DR. DREYFUSS) That's who we had the fight about—Miss Olson—you know, the other girl who just left—

DR. DREYFUSS You ought to print programs.

FRAN (*Pushing the coffee away*) I'm so tired. Please —just let me sleep.

DR. DREYFUSS Not tonight, little girl. (*Shakes her*) Come on, Fran, open your eyes. You mustn't sleep now. (*To* CHUCK) All right, give me a hand. Now comes the dangerous part.

CHUCK (*Concerned*)　What do you mean, dangerous?

DR. DREYFUSS　We gotta walk her around a couple of hours. I have to be careful I don't get a heart attack. (*He lifts* FRAN *up on her feet*) All right, Fran, we're going for a nice little walk . . . all around the apartment. (CHUCK *stands there watching*) You're just going to stand there, God's gift to women?

CHUCK　What should I do?

DR. DREYFUSS　Take her other arm. In this neighborhood I don't like to walk alone. (CHUCK *takes her other arm; they continue walking as the lights fade into a blackout. Five* A.M.: *Through the windows we can see the first faint light of dawn.* FRAN, *in her slip, is asleep on the bed.* DR. DREYFUSS *and* CHUCK, *both on the sofa, sit exhausted, their legs outstretched. Neither one seems to have the strength to speak*) If I charged you by the mile, I'd be a rich man today.

CHUCK　The color's come back to her cheeks. Don't you think she has better color?

DR. DREYFUSS (*He glances at her*)　If you happen to like green, yes.

CHUCK (*He gets up and looks at her*)　But she'll be okay, won't she?

DR. DREYFUSS　She'll sleep on and off for the next twenty-four hours. Then she'll have a headache so bad they'll complain on Sixty-fourth Street . . . This will be followed by a monumental depression because we saved her life

. . . In between this there'll be constant throwing up
. . . All in all, she won't make the perfect house guest
. . . Hold on to the good china, I'm gonna try to stand
up.
(*He struggles to his feet*)

CHUCK You okay?

DR. DREYFUSS I'll have to wear braces the rest of my life.
Fortunately I got a brother in surgical supplies . . . Let
me have another cup of lousy coffee.

CHUCK (*He brings over the coffee*) I don't know what
I would have done without you, Doc.

DR. DREYFUSS (*Reaching in his bag*) Probably you would
have picked up a third girl and I'd be here pumping
Miss Olson too. (*He takes out a pad and pen*) How do
you spell her last name?

CHUCK Who?

DR. DREYFUSS (*Looks at him, then points to* FRAN) This
one. Why, what have you got in the kitchen?

CHUCK Oh. Kubelik . . . With two K's.
(CHUCK *stares at him*)

DR. DREYFUSS Where does she live?

CHUCK You don't have to report this, do you, Doc?

DR. DREYFUSS You ever hear of a thing called "police regu-
lations"?

CHUCK But she didn't mean it. It was . . . it was an accident.

DR. DREYFUSS (*Looking at him*) She tripped over the bottle and the pills fell in her mouth? What do you mean, an accident?

CHUCK I mean, she had too much to drink . . . she didn't know what she was doing . . . there was no suicide note or anything . . . Believe me, Doc, I'm not thinking about myself . . .

DR. DREYFUSS (*Mockingly*) Perish the thought.

CHUCK It's just that she's got a family . . . and there's the people in the office . . . the company . . . please, Doc, just look at her . . . She's really a wonderful girl . . .

DR. DREYFUSS (*He looks at* CHUCK, *then at the sleeping* FRAN) Well, as a doctor I guess I can't prove it *wasn't* an accident . . .

CHUCK Thanks, Doc.

DR. DREYFUSS (*He closes the pad*) But as another human being, don't walk up the same staircase I'm walking down! (*He picks up his bag, puts it on the table, packs and closes it*) You kids today think you can get away with anything. You don't care who you hurt as long as you have yourself a good time . . . Well, life doesn't work that way, believe me.

CHUCK I found that out, Doc.

DR. DREYFUSS (*Stops at the door*) And don't think just

because I'm the older generation, I don't know what's going on. Experimentally, I took a trip on LSD.

CHUCK   You did?

DR. DREYFUSS   I had a better time in Miami Beach when it rained for two weeks . . .

> (*He exits and* CHUCK *closes the door behind him.* CHUCK *crosses back into the room, behind the bed where* FRAN *is fast asleep. He pulls the cover around her. Then he gets his coat, fishes out the Christmas card from* SHELDRAKE. *He turns and looks at the audience*)

CHUCK   Look, I'd like to say something on her behalf . . . Aside from one tiny illicit affair and one very unprofessional suicide attempt . . . there lies one of the most decent girls it's been my privilege to meet.

> (*He takes the phone to the coffee table, sits on the table and starts to dial. An overhead spotlight comes up as* CHUCK *dials his phone.* VOICES *sing in the orchestra pit*)

VOICES

> Christmas Day is here and so are we,
> Time for children and presents
> And Christmas tree happiness.

> (VOICES *continue humming as* SHELDRAKE *steps into the spotlight answering a phone which he carries*)

SHELDRAKE   Yes?

CHUCK (*On his own phone in his apartment. Softly*) It's me, Mr. Sheldrake. Chuck Baxter. I hate to disturb you but something important's come up . . . I think it would be a good idea if you could see me . . . at the apartment . . . as soon as possible . . .

SHELDRAKE　On Christmas morning? What's this all about, Baxter?

CHUCK　I didn't want to tell you over the phone . . . but that certain party. You know who I mean . . . I found her here last night . . . she'd taken an overdose of sleeping pills.

SHELDRAKE　*What?*

HELEN SHELDRAKE (*Appears next to* SHELDRAKE)　What is it, Jeff? Anything wrong?

SHELDRAKE (*He covers the phone*)　One of our employees had an accident. Nothing serious. (*Into the phone*) How bad is it?

CHUCK　Well, it was touch-and-go there for a while, but she's sleeping it off now . . . I thought you might like to be here when she wakes up . . .

SHELDRAKE　Well—of course I would—but I just can't get away . . . Listen, do you think there'll be any er . . . problems . . . I mean, with a doctor?

CHUCK　No, he's a friend of mine and I kept your name out of it . . . So I think you're in the clear, trouble-wise.

SHELDRAKE　Don't think I don't appreciate that, Baxter.

CHUCK　Well, you know me. Loyal and resourceful . . .

SHELDRAKE　And if you need anything, medicines, well, you know, I'll pay for everything.

CHUCK Right. I'll just put it on the bill with the Tom and Jerries . . . Is there any sort of message you want me to give her?

SHELDRAKE A message. Like what?

CHUCK Never mind. I'll think of something . . . Good-by, Mr. Sheldrake. (*He hangs up; the lights black out on* CHUCK *but remain on* SHELDRAKE)

SHELDRAKE Good-by, Baxter . . . and I really apprecia—
(*He realizes* CHUCK *has hung up. He puts down the phone, stands for a second, then exits. The* VOICES *sing*)

VOICES
If Christmas Day is really in your heart
You don't have to save up all your love
To give once a year.
Try to give, learn to live
Each day like Christmas Day.

(*It is later that morning.* FRAN *moves in the bed.* CHUCK *enters with a tablecloth to set the table. He looks at her*)

CHUCK Good morning.
(*He closes the door*)

FRAN (*She holds her hands over her eyes*) You wanna bet?

CHUCK (*Looking out the window*) Actually good afternoon. You slept all day. It looks like snow.

FRAN I don't think I could stand the noise.
(*She props herself a bit, not without discomfort*)

CHUCK Fresh Colombian coffee coming right up, each bean carefully selected by El Exigente himself.

FRAN (*She looks at him*) I didn't know this was your apartment . . . I'm sorry . . .

CHUCK You'll be a lot sorrier in a few minutes. I make the world's worst coffee—

FRAN I'm so ashamed. Why didn't you just let me die?

CHUCK (*He moves toward her*) Hey, what kind of talk is that? You were just emotionally distressed again. So instead of getting hiccups, you took a few sleeping pills . . .
(*He puffs up her pillow. The front door opens and* DR. DREYFUSS *enters*)

DR. DREYFUSS Anything unusual?

CHUCK (*He turns to him*) No. She's resting.

DR. DREYFUSS I meant with you. I expected to find six naked dancing girls feeding you grapes. (*He crosses to* FRAN, *lifts her hand to take her pulse. She looks at him*) Good afternoon. Remember me?

FRAN (*She turns to him*) Yeah. You slapped me in the face last night.

DR. DREYFUSS (*To* CHUCK) A bedside manner I never had. (*Lets go* FRAN's *arm*) If that's your pulse, I'm not crazy about it.

FRAN I'm alive. Doesn't that make you happy? What do I owe you?

DR. DREYFUSS (*Looking at the thermometer*) For your recovery, nothing. For my recovery, you couldn't afford it.
(*Shakes the thermometer*)

FRAN Sure I can. I'm rich. I've got a hundred dollars here someplace. Where's my bag? (*She reaches into her purse and takes out the one hundred dollar bill*) Take it, Doctor. A hundred dollars is the going price for me these days.

DR. DREYFUSS (*Putting a thermometer in her mouth and crossing to flick ashes on the coffee table*) Use it to stock up on Campbell's soup. What you need is hot food and plenty of rest.

FRAN What I need is to be left alone. What's the world coming to when a person can't get off whenever he wants?

DR. DREYFUSS (*Crossing to the foot of the bed*) Shame on you. Shame on you for being young and pretty and sorry you're alive. I'm a general practitioner. You want sympathy, go to a specialist.

CHUCK She's just tired, Doc.

DR. DREYFUSS I don't know. No one today can take heartache any more. Where I was brought up, as a kid we got *misery* as a reward. Like I tell the people with gallstones, live with it a few days. It'll pass.

FRAN (*Looks at DR. DREYFUSS, a faint smile*) Thanks for the poetry, Doctor.

DR. DREYFUSS (*Mock heart attack*) Don't tell me, is that

the beginning of a smile I see? Well, don't let it lay there like a lump on your lips, give birth to it. Give me a full-grown, healthy smile. The way I walked for you last night I deserve it.

FRAN   I'm sorry, Doctor, it's the best I can do.

DR. DREYFUSS   Then take my advice. (*He sings "A Young Pretty Girl Like You"*)

> Put my glasses on on the top of your head
> On the top of your head—you won't see a thing
> And the less you see, the sooner you'll be
> Smiling, laughing, and happy.

CHUCK   (*Singing*)

> Oh yes, the less you see the better you feel
> The better you feel, the quicker you smile
> And the quicker you smile, the sooner you'll be happy
> Happy!

DR. DREYFUSS

> And a young pretty girl like you,

CHUCK *and* DR. DREYFUSS

> Pretty as she can be
> Really should be happy,

CHUCK

> Happy.

DR. DREYFUSS

> Try to
> Take my stethoscope, plug it into your ears
> Plug it into your ears—you won't hear a thing.
> When there's too much noise, nobody enjoys
> Smiling, laughing, be happy.

CHUCK *and* DR. DREYFUSS

Oh yes, the less you see, the better you feel
The better you feel, the quicker you smile
And the quicker you smile, the sooner you'll be happy
Happy!

And a young pretty girl like you,

Pretty as she can be
Really should be happy,

CHUCK

Happy.

DR. DREYFUSS

Try to
Open up your mouth, let me look at your throat
Let me look at your throat, don't you say a thing
'Cause the less you say the sooner you'll play
Lipstick, powder, and girl games.

CHUCK *and* DR. DREYFUSS

Oh yes, the less you see, the better you feel
The better you feel, the quicker you smile
And the quicker you smile, the sooner you'll be happy
Happy!

DR. DREYFUSS

And a young pretty girl like you

CHUCK

Why don't you take a look?

CHUCK *and* DR. DREYFUSS

Really should be happy,

CHUCK
> Happy!

CHUCK *and* DR. DREYFUSS
> Yes, a young pretty girl like you
> With all you've been through
> Really should be happy,

DR. DREYFUSS
> Smiling,

CHUCK
> Laughing,

DR. DREYFUSS
> Giggling,

CHUCK *and* DR. DREYFUSS
> Happy!
>> (*At the end of the song,* DR. DREYFUSS *and* CHUCK *are standing, each with one foot on a chair, the other on the table*)

CHUCK   Hey, look, Doc. She's smiling.
> (FRAN *covers her head*)

DR. DREYFUSS   Now I know what Albert Schweitzer felt like. (*He gets his stethoscope and glasses, and begins to leave*) I'll look in again tonight. (*He clutches his heart, breathing hard*) I can't catch my breath . . . Lucky for me I have hospitalization.
> (*He exits.* CHUCK *turns to* FRAN *and looks at her. She looks back at him*)

FRAN   You're not going to keep staring at me like that all day, are you?

CHUCK (*Rising, he crosses to the bookcase*)   I'm sorry. I guess it's the practical nurse in me. Do you play gin?

FRAN   Not well.

CHUCK   Good. If there's anything I love it's a lousy gin rummy player with a hundred dollars. Feet off my table, please. Penny a point?
>   (DOBITCH *and* SYLVIA *enter the stage outside the door of the apartment*)

FRAN   Why do people have to love people anyway?

CHUCK (*Shrugs*)   We just don't know any better, I guess.

FRAN   I read in a science fiction magazine that in the future we won't need love any more. It's going to become an obsolete emotion.

CHUCK   Well, we certainly have a lot to look forward to, don't we? (*Looks at a card*) Do you want that Jack?
>   (*She shakes her head "no"*)

FRAN   Maybe he does love me . . . only he doesn't have the nerve to tell his wife.
>   (*She throws out another card*)

CHUCK   I'm sure that's the explanation.
>   (*He takes the card she threw out*)

FRAN   You really think so?

CHUCK   I really think so.
>   (*She takes another card and throws it out without looking*)

FRAN   I don't . . . Oh, God, I'm so fouled up . . . You're a smart person, Chuck, tell me what to do.

CHUCK   Well—my personal advice is not to throw out that other Jack.

FRAN   (*Distracted*)   I really don't want it.

CHUCK   In that case, I knock with three. You lose.
(*He lays out his cards*)

FRAN   Yeah . . . I guess I do.
(*She turns her head away from him into the pillow and quietly begins to cry again.* CHUCK *looks at her, gets up and pulls the cover over her, knowing she will soon cry herself to sleep.* DOBITCH *and* SYLVIA *are at the door.* DOBITCH *rings.* CHUCK *crosses and opens the door*)

DOBITCH   Four o'clock, kid, aren't you supposed to be in Radio City Music Hall?

CHUCK   (*Trying to keep him out*)   What do you want? You can't come in.

DOBITCH   (*Pushes his way in*)   What's the matter with you? I made a reservation for four o'clock. (CHUCK *closes the door, locking* SYLVIA *out*) "You caught me at the right season, Mr. Dobitch," don't you remember?
(*He sees* FRAN *in bed*)

SYLVIA   Hey, what about me?

DOBITCH   Well, well, well, who'd a thought it. Next time I'll know what to order in the Dining Room.
(DR. DREYFUSS *appears in the vestibule.* CHUCK *and* SYLVIA *speak together*)

CHUCK (*Points to the door*) Get out, Mr. Dobitch.

SYLVIA Hey, come on, what are we waiting for? Open up, willya?

DR. DREYFUSS Mildred, you'll never believe it. (*He enters his apartment*)

CHUCK (*Crosses to the door*) Did you hear what I said, Mr. Dobitch? Get out!

DOBITCH Your problem, kid, is that you run this place like the Long Island Rail Road. You've got schedules but you don't keep to them. (*He hands him a champagne bottle*) Merry Christmas. (*He and* SYLVIA *exit. We hear* DOBITCH *in the vestibule*) Let's go to Central Park.

CHUCK (*Looking at* FRAN) Don't worry. I'll tell them at the office that you were in the neighborhood and you slipped in the snow and came up to dry off . . . and that's maybe the worst story I ever heard.

FRAN But very sweet . . . You know, if I had any brains, Chuck Baxter, I'd have fallen in love with someone nice like you.

CHUCK (*Turns*) Cut it out, Chuck, you'll drive yourself crazy.

FRAN Did I say something wrong?

CHUCK Oh, my gosh, that was really her talking. (*To* FRAN) No, no, you said the rightest thing in the whole world. You couldn't have said anything righter if you tried. (*There is a blackout on the set with a spot remaining on* CHUCK. *He speaks to the audience*) All right, you all heard that. Don't deny it, I was standing right here. She said, "If I had any brains I would have fallen in love with someone nice like you" . . . meaning someone nice like me . . . Oh, I realize the fact that she just tried to kill herself over someone else means my position is still a little shaky . . .

(*Blackout. In a spotlight we see the* THREE EXECS *at a phone*)

KIRKEBY (*On the phone*) Hello, Ginger! Listen, I think I found a spot . . . it's a deserted tug boat on Pier Twenty-three . . . But Ginger . . .
(*He hangs up*)

EICHELBERGER Can't you think of anyplace?

VANDERHOF For crying out loud, will you stop whispering. It's like living with the Goddamned CIA.

EICHELBERGER (*Grabs him*) But tonight was supposed to be my night. What'll we do?

VANDERHOF Take your clammy, oversexed hands off me.

KIRKEBY I don't know, fellas. I'm getting tired of all this. Why don't we just go to a steam bath?

EICHELBERGER Are you crazy? They'd spot the girls there in a minute.

(*Blackout.* FRAN *is in bed;* CHUCK *is helping her into his bathrobe*)

CHUCK Listen, I don't want to seem gloomy, but what are you going to tell your family? About what happened?

FRAN I thought I'd just tell my father. He's hard of

hearing . . . My brother's a problem. He's six-feet-six with a Polish temper.

CHUCK (*Starting to make the bed*) Well, if you need a character reference, I'm your man.

FRAN (*Looks at the guitar on the table*) Is this your guitar?

CHUCK I bought it second-hand three months ago, in another futile attempt to become the life of the party.

FRAN (*Picks it up*) Would you play something for me?

CHUCK In about two weeks. The blisters on my fingers haven't healed yet . . . Luncheon will be served as soon as I finish my housework.

FRAN (*At the sofa with the guitar*) Tell me, how come someone like you isn't married?

CHUCK Oh. Well, there was a girl I wanted to ask back home. Bertha Gosseman. I was so crazy about her I even thought her name was pretty.

FRAN What happened?

CHUCK She married Albert Mangassarian, my best friend. On their wedding day I tried to kill myself.

FRAN You?

CHUCK I was going to hang myself in the attic. My kid sister saved me.

FRAN She cut you down?

CHUCK   No, she wanted to watch, I got embarrassed.
(FRAN *strums the guitar*)

FRAN   Well. I guess there's a lesson in there we've both
learned.

CHUCK   What's that?
(FRAN *and* CHUCK *sing "I'll Never Fall in Love
Again"*)

FRAN

What do you get when you fall in love?
A guy with a pin to burst your bubble
That's what you get for all your trouble.
I'll never fall in love again
I'll never fall in love again.

What do you get when you kiss a guy?
You get enough germs to catch pneumonia
After you do he'll never phone ya.
I'll never fall in love again
I'll never fall in love again.

Don't tell me what it's all about
'Cause I've been there and I'm glad I'm out
Out of those chains
Those chains that bind you
That is why I'm here to remind you.

What do you get when you fall in love?
You only get lies and pain and sorrow
So for at least until tomorrow

FRAN *and* CHUCK

I'll never fall in love again
I'll never fall in love again.

CHUCK

What do you get when you give your heart?
You get it all broken up and battered
That's what you get—a heart that's shattered.
I'll
Never fall in love again,
I'll
Never fall in love again.
Don't tell me what it's all about
'Cause I've been there and I'm glad I'm out
Out of those chains
Those chains that bind you.

FRAN

That is why I'm here to remind you.

FRAN *and* CHUCK

What do you get when you fall in love?
You only get lies and pain and sorrow
So for at least until tomorrow

FRAN

I'll

FRAN *and* CHUCK

Never fall in love again.

CHUCK

I'll

FRAN *and* CHUCK

Never fall in love again
I'll never fall in love again.

FRAN   Are you still in love with Bertha Gosseman?

CHUCK   Well, since she moved to Canada, had six kids and put on forty pounds, my fervor has waned . . . But she sends me a fruit cake every Christmas. We're having it for dessert. And after dessert you know what we're doing?

FRAN   Well, how about going up to White Plains and letting the air out of Mr. Sheldrake's tires?

CHUCK   No, after dessert we're going to finish that gin game . . . (KARL *rings the doorbell;* CHUCK *crosses to the door*) . . . so I want you to keep a clear head. (*Opens the door*) Because I don't want to . . . take advantage of you the way I did yesterday in bed!

FRAN   Karl!

CHUCK   Your brother? . . . How do you do!
    (KARL *walks in menacingly*)

KARL   Get dressed, I got the car downstairs.

FRAN   Karl, how did you find me?

KARL   I went to the office looking for you. Four executives in the Dining Room said I'd find you up here . . . Who's this?

CHUCK (*Friendly*)   My name is C. C. Baxter, Mr. Kubelik, but you can call me Chuck. Can I call you Karl? . . . Ho, heh? . . . Okay . . . Well, Mr. Kubelik, let me say this—

KARL   Get your clothes and let's go.

CHUCK Go where? . . . Oh, he wants you to get your clothes . . . Would Karl care for some coffee and fruit cake? . . .

KARL My advice to you is to shut up. You still got your teeth in your face because I trust my sister. If she tells me nothing went on here, that's good enough for me.

CHUCK Nothing went on here.

KARL Are you my sister?

FRAN Nothing went on here.

KARL That's good enough for me.

FRAN I'll get my clothes.
       (FRAN *goes into the bathroom and closes the door.
       There is an awkward moment as* CHUCK *tries to
       escape the contemptuous gaze of* KARL, *but* KARL
       persists)

CHUCK May I say one thing? . . . Your sister is really *terrific!* (KARL *glares*) No, I think I said the wrong thing . . .
       (*The front door opens and* DR. DREYFUSS *steps in*)

DR. DREYFUSS Hi. How's the patient.

CHUCK Oh. *I'm fine,* Doc.

DR. DREYFUSS I mean Miss Kubelik.

KARL What's the matter with Miss Kubelik?

DR. DREYFUSS   Who are you?

KARL   Her brother.

DR. DREYFUSS (*Takes a step back*)   Oh.

KARL   Who are you?

DR. DREYFUSS   Her doctor. *His* doctor. Just a doctor.

KARL   Why does she need a doctor?

DR. DREYFUSS   Er—ah! (*To* CHUCK) Tell him why she needs a doctor.

CHUCK   Er—fruit cake. Too much fruit cake.

DR. DREYFUSS (*Nods*)   An overdose!

CHUCK   It comes from Canada. And it was a very bad year for Canadian fruit cake.

DR. DREYFUSS   One of their worst.

CHUCK   Oh, what's the use . . . She had an accident.

DR. DREYFUSS   These things happen.

KARL   What things? Hey, what kind of a doctor are you?

DR. DREYFUSS (*Shrugs*)   General practice. Colds, virus—

CHUCK   He gave her a shot and pumped her stomach out.

KARL   What for?
   (FRAN *comes out of the bathroom*)

FRAN   Because I took some sleeping pills. But I'm all right now. So let's go.

KARL   Not until I find out what went on here. Why did you take sleeping pills?

CHUCK   On . . . on account of me. (KARL *looks at him*) I jilted her. I threw her over. (*He smiles at* FRAN, *pleased with himself. Then turns to* KARL) You're going to hit me, aren't you?

KARL   You know it, brother.
   (KARL *smashes his fist into* CHUCK's *stomach.* CHUCK *groans and stands there doubled over*)

FRAN   Karl! (*Then* KARL *finishes the job, smashing his fist into* CHUCK's *jaw, who goes sprawling across the room, over a chair and onto the floor*) Stop it! Leave him alone.

DR. DREYFUSS (*Looking on*)   Tell me if you're going to do that again. I want my wife to watch.

FRAN (*Rushes to* CHUCK *on the floor*)   You idiot. You really are an idiot!

KARL (*Opens the door*)   Let's go.

FRAN   Good-by, idiot!
   (*She kisses him warmly on the cheek and exits*)

DR. DREYFUSS (*Bends down, looks at* CHUCK) You know, Baxter, I was just thinking. If I had three more like you in the building, I could give up the rest of my practice.
> (FRAN *and* KARL *exit from the stoop. The* EXECS *emerge after them, dancing and singing*)

We did the right thing, the proper thing,
What else were we to do?

If it was your sister,
I'd do the same for you.

> (*A* YOUNG MAN *crosses in front of them*)

YOUNG MAN   Happy New Year, Mr. Vanderhof.

VANDERHOF   Happy New Year, kid.
> (YOUNG MAN *continues off and exits*)

DOBITCH   Who's that?

VANDERHOF   A new boy in my department.

DOBITCH   Single?

VANDERHOF   Yeah.

DOBITCH   With his own apartment?

VANDERHOF   Yeah.
> (*They all look at each other, then dance off in the direction of the* YOUNG MAN *as they sing*)

We did the right thing, the proper thing,
What else was there to do?
> (*They exit*)

Blackout

Scene 3

The lights go up on SHELDRAKE'S *office at the left.*
SHELDRAKE *enters and crosses to his desk; he looks at the*
papers and calls offstage.

SHELDRAKE   Miss Olson . . . (*No answer . . . a little*
louder) *Miss Olson.* (MISS OLSON *enters, carrying a sheet*
of paper with a check attached. He seems perturbed)
I'm not taking you away from anything, am I?

MISS OLSON   I'm sorry, I was just typing this up. (*She*
puts it on his desk) It needs your signature. (*He looks*
at it) By the way, shall I tell the cashier to dock Miss
Kubelik's pay? She didn't come in today. (*He looks up at*
her) Virus, do you think?

SHELDRAKE   I don't know what you're implying, but I've
been with my family for the past two nights. In addition
to which I don't think it's any of your business.
      (*He signs the check and paper*)

MISS OLSON   I know, just typing, filing, and reserving
you hotel space in Atlantic City . . . or is it West Sixty-
seventh Street now?

SHELDRAKE (*Glances at her*)   I think that'll be all, Miss
Olson.

MISS OLSON   You know what's going to happen to you

some day? You're going to use up all the girls in the office . . . and you'll have to turn to IBM machines . . . That means you'll have to get a bigger car, Mr. Sheldrake.

SHELDRAKE   The Christmas party is over. I think you'd better pull yourself together.

MISS OLSON   You know . . . somehow I could adjust to the end of our affair by telling myself I still had a good-paying job. But I think when you tell that kid your interoffice fling is over she's going to head for the nearest gas pipe. She's not made of concrete like me.

SHELDRAKE (*Gets up*)   I've got a conference now. I think we'd better finish this discussion later.

MISS OLSON   If you enjoy talking to yourself, because I won't be here. I'm quitting as a Christmas present to myself. (*She picks up the papers from his desk*) You just signed my two weeks' severance pay.

SHELDRAKE (*Looks at her*)   That's up to you, Peggy.
        (*He starts to go*)

MISS OLSON   Oh . . . In case you're worrying about anyone telling your wife about all this, I have one word of advice . . . worry.
        (*He glares at her; the lights go off on the office set. He turns and exits*)

Blackout

The lights go up on CHUCK *outside Lum Ding's Chinese Restaurant.* CHUCK *takes a note from his pocket, shows it, and addresses the audience.*

CHUCK (*Reads*) "Would like to have a drink with you five o'clock, Lum Ding's Restaurant . . . J. S. Sheldrake" . . . (*Puts the note in his pocket*) . . . Well, I can see a two-week vacation with pay coming up for being loyal, cooperative and pretty damned quiet about Christmas Eve . . . I wasn't going to come except I have something to say myself . . . How does this sound to you? Be honest. (*Clears his throat*) "Mr. Sheldrake, inasmuch as you seem to be in an inextricable position, to relieve you of any further pain or hardship, since you don't really want her anyway and I do, I would like to take Miss Kubelik off your hands . . . It would be the thing to do . . . solution-wise" . . . I like that—"inextricable"—(*He turns and goes into the restaurant, which lights up as he enters. It is decorated for New Year's Eve, although it's only about 5:00 P.M.* CHUCK *crosses to* SHELDRAKE *at the usual table*) Happy New Year, Mr. Sheldrake.

SHELDRAKE Hello, Baxter. Sit down. Can I get you anything?

CHUCK No, thanks. I'm on my way to someone's party.

SHELDRAKE Pretty?

CHUCK Well, if you like chunky middle-aged doctors.

He's got a few interns that are anxious to meet me . . . Er, Mr. Sheldrake . . . inasmuch as you seem to be in an inextricable position—

SHELDRAKE But I'm not. At least not any more. If you were in the office about eight-fifteen this morning, you would have seen me arrive with two large suitcases.

CHUCK Going somewhere, sir?

SHELDRAKE Temporarily to the New York Athletic Club. Mrs. Sheldrake and I have split up—

CHUCK You mean—for good?

SHELDRAKE It's funny what can happen to a twelve-year-old marriage with one phone call from a jealous ex-secretary.

CHUCK Oh. I'm sorry.

SHELDRAKE So it looks like I'll be taking Miss Kubelik off your hands permanently. By the way, I'm not ungrateful for Christmas Eve. I was thinking about a two-week vacation, with pay.

CHUCK (*Empty*) Gee, I never expected that.

SHELDRAKE Anyway, I'm meeting Fran—Miss Kubelik— later tonight. I intend asking her to marry me.

CHUCK I see. Well, I guess you don't need any good luck, knowing how she feels about you. I'm sure you'll both be very happy.

SHELDRAKE I appreciate that, Baxter, especially after the

way I must have sounded on the phone the other day. I imagine I impressed you as a Class A-One heel.

CHUCK   Well, it's not my place—

SHELDRAKE   It's all right. You can be honest.

CHUCK   Okay. That was my impression. Class A-One heel.

SHELDRAKE   I don't blame you, Baxter. My behavior that day was anything but admirable. But you understood, I couldn't help myself. My hands were tied.

CHUCK   Well, maybe it was the kicking with your feet that I objected to.

SHELDRAKE   I'll let that pass, Baxter. We've all been under a big strain this past week.

CHUCK   That's very charitable of you, sir. I'll try to keep my place from now on . . . So, when is the happy day?

SHELDRAKE   Well, I'm not sure.

CHUCK   I mean, this week? This month? This year?

SHELDRAKE   I said I'm not sure. You know, these things—

CHUCK   (Nods) —usually drag out for months . . .

SHELDRAKE   That's right. They usually drag out for months.

CHUCK   There's always a million details—

SHELDRAKE   Exactly. All those damn details—

CHUCK And in the meantime you have no place to go with Miss Kubelik, so you'd like the key to my apartment again.

SHELDRAKE Well, I can't very well take her into the New York Athletic Club. And it's New Year's Eve, there's not a hotel room in town. So if I could just have it for tonight—

CHUCK (*Puts a key on the table*) Here you are, Mr. Sheldrake.

SHELDRAKE (*Picks it up*) Thanks, Baxter. (CHUCK *gets up*) I'm sorry to ask on such short notice but I didn't know until last night that Mrs. Sheldrake—Hey, Baxter, wait a minute. You gave me the wrong key. This is for the Executive Bathroom.

CHUCK Right, Mr. Sheldrake. I'm all washed up around here.

SHELDRAKE What are you talking about?

CHUCK You're not going to bring anybody up to my apartment.

SHELDRAKE I'm not bringing anybody—I'm bringing Miss Kubelik.

CHUCK (*Leans forward, his voice rising*) *Especially* Miss Kubelik!

SHELDRAKE Just a minute, Baxter. I've been pretty damn nice to you. You were handing me that key fast enough when you were getting raises and promotions in the other hand.

CHUCK Mr. Sheldrake, I refuse to work for a man who would make a Junior Executive out of anyone whose only qualification is an available *eighty-six fifty a month apart-ment* . . . Especially when that Junior Executive is hypo-critical, opportunistic, and an indiscriminate streetwalker *like me!* HAPPY NEW YEAR! (*He storms out of the restaurant into the street. Lights dim on the restaurant.* CHUCK *speaks to the audience*) I will NEVER—never, never, never, EVER get myself into a situation like that again. *That's* a promise! Oh, God, there's that word again! (*He sings*)

> Promises, promises,
> I'm all through with promises, promises now.
> I don't know how
> I got the nerve to walk out.
> If I shout
> Remember I feel free.
> Now I can look at myself and be proud
> I'm laughing out loud.
> Oh, promises, promises,
> This is where those promises, promises end.
> I won't pretend
> That what was wrong can be right.
> Every night I'll sleep now.
> No more lies.
> Things that I promised myself fell apart
> But I found my heart.
> Promises, their kind of promises
> Can just destroy your life.
> Oh, promises, those kind of promises
> Take all the joy from life.
> Oh, promises, promises, my kind of promises
> Can lead to joy and hope and love,
> Yes, love.
>   (*He exits*)

Blackout

Scene 5

The voices of TWO COUPLES *are heard as they climb the steps to the vestibule.*

INTERN   Hey, Doc, where are you. We're here! This is the place.

DR. DREYFUSS (*Appearing at the door*)   Mildred, they're here.
> (*The* TWO COUPLES *enter* DR. DREYFUSS'S *apartment*)

DR. DREYFUSS (*To the last* INTERN)   Where's the ice? You were supposed to bring ice.
> (*Enters his apartment. In his apartment,* CHUCK *is packing his clothes into a suitcase. He looks up and sees the audience*)

CHUCK   I'll be leaving in a few minutes so I guess I won't be seeing you any more . . . You've been very patient . . . Listen, my rent is paid up for the next two weeks, so if you need a place to stay—you know where to find the key.
> (DR. DREYFUSS'S *door opens across the hall*)

INTERN (*Offstage*)   Where you going, Doc.

DR. DREYFUSS   Be right back. (CHUCK *continues packing.* DR. DREYFUSS *comes in*) Hello, Baxter. You were supposed to come to my party and we're running short of ice so I thought I'd come to a professional. (*Looks around, whispers*) Who's playing tonight?

CHUCK   It's okay, Doc. I'm alone.

DR. DREYFUSS   On New Year's Eve? Don't kid me. Ten-to-twelve I'll be in here on another house call.

CHUCK   (*Hands him a bottle*) There's no ice, Doc. I defrosted the refrigerator . . . Can you use a bottle of champagne?

DR. DREYFUSS   Booze we don't need. Why don't you join us, Baxter? I got a psychiatrist, a cardiologist and a gynecologist, all right up your alley.

CHUCK   Thanks, but I've got to finish packing. I'm moving out tonight.

DR. DREYFUSS   Moving out? You mean giving up the apartment? Where are you going?

CHUCK   I'm not sure yet. All I know is I got to get out of this place.

DR. DREYFUSS   Mildred'll be sorry to hear it. Once you moved in, she gave up the Late Show . . .

CHUCK   Doc, in case I don't see you again . . . I just want to thank you for taking care of that girl.

DR. DREYFUSS   Forget it. She looked like a nice kid. I wouldn't trust her with a bottle of aspirins, but a nice kid. Whatever happened to her?

CHUCK   Oh, you know me when it comes to women. Easy

come, easy go . . . (*We see* FRAN *come down the vestibule toward* CHUCK's *apartment*) . . . Come on, Doc. Let's kill the bottle for old-time's sake.
>   (*He pulls the cork, it pops with a loud bang.* FRAN *freezes at the door*)

FRAN   Oh, my God! *Mr. Baxter!!* (*She rushes to the door*) *Mr. Baxter!!!* (*She opens the door and rushes into the apartment as* CHUCK *stands there pouring champagne into* DR. DREYFUSS's *glass* . . . CHUCK *looks up and sees* FRAN) Oh!

CHUCK   Miss Kubelik . . . What's wrong?

FRAN   Nothing. I heard an explosion and I thought—well, I thought that—that you did something terrible.

CHUCK   Like what?

FRAN   Like leaving town without calling me.

CHUCK   I *am* leaving town and I didn't see much point in calling.

FRAN   Try me.

CHUCK   What's that?

FRAN   I said try me.

CHUCK   Hello? Is Miss Kubelik there? . . . I'd like to speak to Miss Kubelik, please . . . Fran?
>   (*They just stare at each other, as if in a trance, almost oblivious to the fact that* DR. DREYFUSS *is standing there between them. He looks at* FRAN)

DR. DREYFUSS It's for you.

FRAN Yes, Chuck? . . .

CHUCK I just wanted to say good-by . . . and wish you and Mr. Sheldrake all the happiness in the world.

FRAN What was that name again? My Eustachian tubes are closing up.

DR. DREYFUSS What did I tell you? It's not even ten-to-twelve yet.

CHUCK Mr. Sheldrake told me he was meeting you tonight to ask you to marry him.

FRAN He did?

CHUCK . . . What did you say?

FRAN What do you think I said?

DR. DREYFUSS (*Looks at* CHUCK, *then at* FRAN. *There is a pause*) I can't stand it! What did you say?

FRAN It suddenly hit me for the first time. Mr. Sheldrake and I don't have anything in common. He really doesn't like basketball.

CHUCK (*Big smile*) He doesn't?

DR. DREYFUSS Who could marry anyone who doesn't like basketball? (*To* CHUCK) I'm glad you're not moving out. I'm getting used to you. Happy New Year . . . I said

Happy— (*He waves his arm in disgust and exits*) Forget it, Mildred, he's busy again.

> (DR. DREYFUSS *goes through the vestibule, into his apartment, and closes the door.* CHUCK *and* FRAN *have virtually been staring at each other all this time.* FRAN *picks up the deck of cards on the table, sits on the sofa and starts to deal as* CHUCK *stares at her*)

CHUCK (*Crosses to her right*)   I love you, Miss Kubelik.

FRAN   You'll have to speak louder. You want the Queen of Hearts?

CHUCK (*Sitting right of her, picks up his cards*)   I said, Miss Kubelik, that I absolutely adore you.

FRAN   I heard you. Now shut up and play cards.
(*MUSIC swells*)

CURTAIN

DATE DUE

MAY 1 '72			
MAY 15 '73			
DEC 1			
GAYLORD			PRINTED IN U.S.A.